seaweed and eat it

a family foraging

and cooking

adventure

Fiona Houston and Xa Milne

Virgin BOOKS

First published in Great Britain in 2008 by
Virgin Books Ltd
Thames Wharf Studios
Rainville Road
London
W6 9HA

A catalogue record for this book is available from the British Library.

ISBN 978 0 7535 1341 5

Designed by Virgin Books Ltd

Printed and bound by CPI MacKays

All photographs courtesy of Fiona Houston and Xa Milne, except: pages 6, 11, 17, 46, 47, 48, 78, 98, 118, 121, 138, 140, 148, 149, 160, 165, 166 © Chris Watt, www. chriswatt.com; pages 143, 145, 152, 153 (top), 154, 155, 156, 157 (top), 158 © David Mitchel, Northern Ireland Fungus Group; pages 51, 52 M.J. Younger; page 176 © William Milliken, page 42, 56 © iStockphoto, page 114 © Susan Steel, Irish Sea Fisheries Board.

All illustrations © Olivia Doherty, www.oliviadoherty.com

CONTENTS

To our fathers

Adair Houston, 3 June 1926–5 May 2003

Gavin Younger, 3 June 1926–3 September 2003

With love and appreciation

FOREWORD BY AA GILL

Years ago, before either of us had families, Xa and I spent a summer in Scotland cooking. I was supposed to be teaching local stuff, and Xa and a couple of others, including Hugh Fearnley-Whittingstall, were supposed to be learning something. Actually, we all hung out in a big old kitchen making a mess, producing heroic amounts of fantastically energetic, robust and occasionally inspired food, to feed each other and anyone else who put their head through the back door.

Even after all the years and all the dinners, I can remember some marvellous soups: Parton Bree, made with little green crabs discarded from the bottom of lobster creels – Hugh made a rather piss-elegant version with local langoustines; Braw Bree from a hare off the hill; Scotch broth with prunes; Cranachan with soft fruit from the kitchen garden.

The point was to source as many ingredients as possible from one glen. I shot a fat stag in the heather, caught brown trout, made the others dig tatties and kale, walked up blaeberries. I went to see Peggy Mackenzie, a retired keeper's wife, who agreed to teach me how to make haggis in exchange for a couple of rabbits. With the softest of voices and the gentlest fingers, she showed me how to make haggis from the pluck of the little four-horned Harris sheep, whose blood made black puddings, and whose delicate legs we salted. I baked on an ancient stove: boiled cakes, drappit scones and slow-baked rhubarb jam flavoured with cloves, and a great peppery black bun. In the kitchen we made Crowdie, scented with wild garlic, and ate it with warm farls of oatcakes.

Very quickly the food and the place became indistinguishable, merged into one thing. Cooking and walking, stalking and digging, tying a hook and pricking your thumbs for brambles, all came together as part of a single experience. It was one of my happiest summers cooking – an Arcadian month or two.

Xa and Fiona have now produced this wonderfully practical, bountiful and inspiring book, giving not just a sense of place and season, but adventure to what our children eat. When we did it twenty years ago, it was for fun; today it is still fun, but it contains a more important message of care and connection to the land and ingredients. Most food books begin at the end of the gathering process; this one, quite rightly, starts at the beginning. I love it not least for its reminder of the taste of a happy late summer in the Highlands.

Adrian Gill, 2007

1 BACK TO OUR ROOTS

Seaweed and Eat It is the result of a serendipitous meeting in a primary school playground of two women with a love of food and the outdoors, and a large quota of maternal guilt that our children might grow up with no real connection to the countryside and where their food comes from. We wanted to create, for our families, some adventurous memories of childhood, like we were lucky enough to have, and instil a love of fresh food and cooking along the way.

We hope you take this book as a recipe for outdoor fun and informal eating, whether you have kids, or are just a kid at heart, whether you are rekindling childhood memories, or are taking your first foraging steps beyond buying elderflower cordial in the supermarket.

FIONA

At the time, it seemed like every evening after school, my mother would use her child labour force of four to pick an industrial amount of brambles to make a year's supply of bramble jelly. Harvesting the mushrooms from the field in front of our house felt like Christmas had come early; we made vats of delicious buttery, creamy mushroom soup that my father would swoon over. The standing stake nets on the tidal mud flats of the Solway Firth were another opportunity for foraged food. We waited until the fishermen had cleared the nets of salmon and sea trout, then went in and collected from the muddy shallows the flounder that were not deemed worthy of eating. My mother, who has lived her whole life on the same farm, instilled in us a sense of place, and her no-nonsense practicality will always be that little voice in the back of my head, telling us to just get outside and get on with it, and we'll rustle up good food however many friends show up in the kitchen at meal times.

That flounder was, looking back on it, real food to me; picked fresh and brought home to fry up, not the fancy food heavy on cream and sauces I learnt on a summer cooking course my mother forced me to go on, thinking that I would never bag a husband unless I knew how to make mayonnaise by hand. Her insurance policy backfired when I increased a dress size in just three months; she didn't realise that she had given me all the culinary education I needed.

Anyway, we all left home, no more bramble picking or mushroom soup, we didn't really pick much of anything other than picking up take-away Chinese. My husband, Duncan, shared a similar childhood to me, school holidays spent tramping the Irish countryside with his mother and his Irish relations, in search of fish, mushrooms and frockens. My mother-in-law, Charlotte, used to love my reaction when she told me childhood stories of shooting starlings with an airgun then eating them after roasting them on the fire.

We spent a decade living in Washington DC, getting increasingly frustrated with the peaches from Super Fresh, the local supermarket, that were anything but super fresh; they went mouldy in the fruit bowl before they ripened. Where were those famous Georgia peaches, rosy and sweet, still warm from the sun?

Despite our frequent wilderness camping trips in the Rocky Mountains and on an island in the St Lawrence River, my foraging tendencies were put in the cold storage part of my brain in my quest to climb my way up the journalistic ladder. Our lives were focused on conspiracy theories and policy platforms, not wild garlic and blossoms. Then, one spring, I flew home and set out for a dog walk along the river with my sister.

Val stoops to pick some green leaves on the riverbank. 'What is that?' I ask, embarrassed at my ignorance.

'Wild garlic,' comes the reply.

'Oh, really? That's what it looks like,' I reply. 'I've always wondered.' Pause. 'I can't believe I didn't know that!'

Maybe it was sibling rivalry that sparked my curiosity, but it was time for us to get back to our roots. Time to make sure that our children would not be consigned to thinking rock-hard, mouldy peaches was the norm, or that all vegetables came wrapped in cling film, not dirt.

In August, we went for a walk along the beach with our American friend, Andrew, and his Chinese friend, Wei. Her eyes were fixed on the forests of kelp dancing in the waves at low tide.

'Wow. Look at all that seaweed. Don't you eat it?'

Actually, no, we don't. But why not? And that's what got me thinking.

Later that year, still suffering cultural re-entry shock in a school playground in Edinburgh, Xa and I somehow got talking. We started comparing notes about terrible summers; we had both just lost our fathers. We discovered that they shared the same birthday, 3 June 1926, and, we later discovered, had been friends in the army just after the war. Serendipity.

So we got talking, one June morning, sipping mint tea in my back garden, comparing memories of recently lost fathers and parental responsibilities and good food.

XA

As a young child, I ate my way through the seasons, starting with red and white wild strawberries, which grew by the garden gate. I liked eating them when they were warm and sun-ripened, and nobody was looking. I would walk many a mile down the lanes, searching for yellow rasps, wild gooseberries and red currants, which we would later dip in egg white, then icing sugar. One of my favourite snacks was sucking the sweet nectar out of the honeysuckle flowers. It wasn't just the bees that were rivals for the sugar on offer, my younger brother knew about this fructose supply, so at all times I employed stealth tactics when loitering at the end of the garden. The only evidence I'd been there would be a pile of flower heads thrown carelessly on the ground, discarded like sweetie papers. Later, I would search for blaeberries and brambles and look forward to rose-hip syrup in the mornings, which meant winter was on its way.

I did have some guidance as a child – nature studies was my favourite subject at primary school, I loved making casts of spring twigs, or working out what exact shade of blue the egg shell was. Finding a special object for the nature table was a constant quest and helped me notice what was around me. My father was good on trees and fish, my grandmother, meanwhile, was a botanist, grasses being her area of expertise. They both tried to steer me towards a greater knowledge and appreciation of the plant world. It was only when they both died that I realised what went with them.

As my three young boys grew up, I realised that they only had Simon and I to show them the wonders of the outdoor world. We both had fond but hazy memories of gorging ourselves on berries as children, but, as an urban family, we had become totally detached from growing things and the awareness of the seasons. The children had recently invested in a four-player handset for the PlayStation and the future generally looked quite bleak. Even the dog was beginning to look overweight.

One Sunday, as Simon set off to the local shop to buy some thyme, to flavour our joint of pork, I stopped him just in time, because all the while it was growing unrecognised, in our back garden. Meanwhile, I staggered past my decorative espaliered apple trees, laden down with bags of Granny Smiths from the supermarket – barely registering that I had a fine crop myself.

A cup of tea with fellow-mum, Fiona, confirmed the fact that the world was indeed demented, and had been for as long as we could remember. She picked the mint leaves from her own plant to make her brew from. It struck me as being very simple and uncomplicated. You pick a leaf, it grows back.

You use a tea bag, the box empties. This started a train of thought. How do you find plants like camomile and wild thyme? I've been buying linden blossom tea bags for ten years now and presumably I walk under lime trees all the time? I knew I had to do some blue-sky thinking fast.

The beginning of the journey, from bush to cup, plant to plate; a shared dream, where we could let the children go wild, get dirty and re-connect with nature. We proposed a year of family foraging and cooking, to find out how to find, pick and eat with confidence. Most of all, we want to encourage people to get back into the outdoor garden and feel safe.

We hope we have made it clear and fun, and that we can open up the edible treasure hunt to a wider audience.

The children have complained, they have gone on strike, they have wailed at being under attack from midges, they have got muddy and wet and got stung. But we have all had a great year. Some of the high points, as listed by the kids: learning how to make fire; smearing blueberries on their faces; eating strange things; identifying things; eating bramble ice cream; fighting with sticks; making dens; camp-fire stories; s'mores; picking, making and drinking camomile tea; drinking strawberry and elderflower cordial; making gnocchi out of nettles; eating sorrel; wild garlic bread; more family time. Some of our high points: blaeberry smoosh; dandelion salad; discovering seaweed; the list is endless. And that's the point. There is no need to stop, the seasons roll on, bringing new offerings to our plate and we would be foolish not to help ourselves.

back to our roots.

2
THE SWEET SMELL OF SPRING

{Nettles, Wild Garlic}

WILD GARLIC

Date: *20 March 2007*
Weather: *Cold, watery sun*
Place: *Riverbank*
Objective: *To inhale the Sweet Smell of Spring*

We emerge from a winter of hibernation with small tentative steps. Is winter really over? The light is pale, the sun watery, birds are ruffling their feathers. The Scottie dog, Jock, has a spring in all four paws. 'About time too,' his jaunty walk says as he explores new smells. The kids are off running along the river path playing tag. We are left swinging our empty bags scanning the hedgerows and looking for a sign that winter is over – a primrose, a celandine, a snowdrop. Anything.

And there it is, a glade of grasshopper-green blades, long and lush – the same shape as its more sedate cousin, lily of the valley. Wild garlic is back. It grows near the river, shaded by trees, a large pool of green, barely a square of earth to be seen. Even Jock rolls on the bouncy, shiny leaves, releasing yet more pungent smells into the damp March air.

Geordie thunders past us, runs off the path, and dives on to the bed of greenery, closely followed in hot pursuit by Lorne and Adair.

'Wow ... this is like falling into a basket of dough balls,' he says. The sweet smell of spring has arrived. Once trodden on, never forgotten.

'Hey, guys, come and try this, it's just like, well ... it is sort of ... really garlicky!' Geordie screeches. The kids come and collapse in the glade, and start pulling up leaves and chewing them. 'This is tasty,' says Lydia, holding a whole bunch up to her nose. 'Mmmmm. Can we make garlic bread, Mum? Please?'

'I thought garlic bread came from the shops, Mum?' says Mungo, happily nibbling on a leaf.

Further down the path, we find drifts of onion grass. We dig with a penknife and see that there are little white bulbs under the earth. We've got food on the brain. We're thinking stir-fry as we inspect the bright green shoots. Later, we find young goose grass for juicing, honey-smelling gorse flower for infusing, young dandelion leaves are starting to sprout, young nettle shoots are out. The promise of things to come.

WILD GARLIC OR RANSOMS

{Allium ursinum}

Wild garlic is an aromatic odyssey, and once you know the smell, there is no turning back. You are – literally – inhaling spring. Just rub the leaves and sniff; the pungent smell really cannot be mistaken for anything else.

Once you have clocked it, it won't leave you alone. Watch where you stamp. Large fields of wild garlic sprout up in woodlands in March like a vibrant green carpet, and it grows in such large quantities that there is no worry about overpicking.

IDENTIFICATION

FIND IT HERE:
Wild garlic grows in damp areas; along the banks of rivers and streams, or in damp, shaded woodland.

WHAT IT LOOKS LIKE:
The leaves are a dark green, broad and spearlike. The delicate white, starlike flowers, also edible, start appearing in April, and last through to June.

commonsense tips.

• Paves from the middle of the plant: they will have the best flavour.

• Once picked, we recommend sealing the leaves in a plastic bag or container; otherwise the garlic smell can be overpowering.

• The leaves have the strongest flavour, but the flowers are an attractive addition to salads, or can be used as a garnish for soup.

WILD GARLIC FOR YOUR HEALTH

Wild garlic has the same properties as cultivated garlic, and has an array of medicinal uses stretching back through the ages and into the modern world. The view that the French smell of garlic may be a common politically incorrect British stereotype, but they have the last laugh – Mediterranean countries have a much lower level of heart disease than the UK, a fact many medical researchers have put down to eating copious amounts of this potent plant.

Some botanists claim that, when it is in season, it has more healthful value than cultivated garlic. Long before the days of endless laboratory testing, ancient medics found that eating garlic was cardio-protective, i.e. good for the long-term health of your circulatory system, good for lowering blood pressure and cholesterol; hence good for preventing heart disease.

All of the 450 allium plants, i.e. all types of onion and garlic, contain protein, and vitamins A and B complex.

A CURE FOR OVER-INDULGENCE?

Nature is kind, it wants to look after us after the holiday party season; all the spring greens act to cleanse the system, and wild garlic is no exception. Alcohol is especially damaging to the liver, but medical research shows that eating garlic helps to neutralise poisons in the liver.

COOKING WITH WILD GARLIC

In early spring, we had so much wild garlic in our kitchens and fridges that our men started pleading with us 'please, no more!' as the smell is overpowering and taints everything else in the fridge – so beware!

Try wild garlic under the skin of chicken, in sandwiches, in sauces, with roast vegetables, and in a loaf of French bread.

Wild garlic leaves can also be used to cook 'en papillote', i.e. the leaves can be wrapped around lamb or fish and grilled or baked.

Try a Cream Cheese and Wild Garlic Dip to eat with carrot or bread sticks: empty a tub of cream cheese into a food processor, add a few wild garlic leaves, a couple of drops of Worcestershire sauce, and blend together.

herb chopper

WILD GARLIC SOUP *Makes 4–6 servings.*

60g/2oz	**BUTTER, OR** 2 tbsp **OIL**
1 medium	**ONION, DICED, OR** 1 handful **ONION GRASS BULBS, FINELY CHOPPED**
2 medium	**POTATOES, DICED**
2 large handfuls	**WILD GARLIC LEAVES** (approximately 340g/12oz)
	SEA SALT AND FRESHLY GROUND BLACK PEPPER
900ml/2 pints	**GOOD VEGETABLE OR CHICKEN STOCK**

1. Heat the butter or oil and gently cook the onion and potatoes until translucent.

2. Add the wild garlic leaves and raise the heat slightly to wilt them.

3. Season the mixture then pour the stock over it.

4. Bring to the boil and simmer until the vegetables are very soft.

5. Liquidise and serve with a spoon of wild garlic pesto or garlic flowers as a garnish.

WILD GARLIC BREAD – KIDS' FAVOURITE!

1 pack	**BUTTER**
2-4 large handfuls	**WILD GARLIC LEAVES**
1 loaf	**CRUSTY BREAD**

1. Keep the butter out of the fridge so that it is soft and easy to spread.

2. Put the garlic leaves in a food processor and chop, then add the butter and mix until leaves are mixed through the butter.

3. Slice the crusty bread three quarters of the way through.

4. Spread the garlic butter on the bread slices, keeping the loaf together.

5. Wrap the bread in foil and bake in a medium-hot oven until the butter has melted through the bread.

6. When serving, slice the bread the whole way through.

WILD GARLIC PESTO *Makes 8–10 servings.*

Wild Garlic Pesto couldn't be easier; just throw everything into a food processor, press the button for a few seconds, and that's it. This pesto is a great addition to the store cupboard, as, once made, it lasts for months. It is great dripped over almost anything: pasta, bread, soup. It is a punchy addition to baked fish or lamb. We used this pesto as a marinade for lamb chops, which we then grilled on the barbecue. If your kids enjoy pesto or garlic bread, they will love this.

Try it mixed into mashed potatoes.

2 large handfuls WILD GARLIC LEAVES
120g/4oz ALMONDS, PINE NUTS OR WALNUTS
EXTRA-VIRGIN OLIVE OIL*
SEA SALT AND FRESHLY GROUND BLACK PEPPER
Juice half A LEMON

1. Put wild garlic leaves, almonds and olive oil in a food processor, then blend until chopped but not completely smooth.
2. Add more olive oil, seasoning and lemon juice to taste.

*Make sure there is enough olive oil to cover the ingredients – the olive oil acts as a preservative – otherwise the pesto will go off.

FOR THE FREEZER

- Garlic butter
- Garlic bread
- Garlic pesto
- Wild garlic leaves, chopped, in olive oil

store cupboard

FOR THE FRIDGE

- Wild garlic pesto can be stored in the fridge for several months, provided it is covered in sufficient olive oil, as can wild garlic leaves without the nuts added

STINGING NETTLES

{*Urtica doica*}

'The sweetly smelling weed'

There is something slightly rebellious about the nettle: maybe that's why we like it so much. It is every gardener's nightmare. But despite all this, it has the audacity to actually taste good and be full of vitamins and trace minerals that are good for you. Of all the green vegetables, including some that we spend hours cultivating in our vegetable gardens or allotments, it is the lowly nettle that comes up trumps on the healthful properties. Nettles have a surprisingly sweet smell and taste, and, in our view, hold up well to any

conventional green vegetable when picked young and fresh. We have found that quickly blanching them in boiling water makes them taste better. During the Second World War, when cultivated vegetables were in short supply, nettles were widely picked and eaten, and it is perhaps because of wartime connotations that eating nettles became such a stigma.

IDENTIFICATION

FIND IT HERE:
Any untended ground – gardens, hedgerows, woodland – in early spring.

WHAT IT LOOKS LIKE:
Nettles are one of the few plants that need
little explanation; most of us have been
stung by a nettle. It is an upright, coarse
perennial that shoots in early spring. The
leaves are heart-shaped and have fine hairs that sting.

WHAT CAN IT BE CONFUSED WITH?:
White and red dead nettle. The non-stinging dead nettles can be dis-
tinguished by the small pink or white flowers that appear on the stem in
springtime, and a square-shaped stem. Dead nettles are also edible, but
don't have the depth of flavour of the stinging nettle.

• The shoots must be picked when young and bright green,
before the nettles become too tall and start to flower.

• Later, in the spring the leaves turn dark green and their
chemical content changes, making them taste bitter.

Commonsense tips.

• Wear gloves when picking nettles – the sting of the leaf lasts until it has
been cooked.

• No need to pick the leaves off the stem – the whole young shoot can be
used.

• If looking for nettles later in the spring, look in shaded woodland where
the shoots may still be young.

• There may be a constant source of young nettles in your local park because the gardeners like to cut nettles to the ground, then the nettles come
back in abundance with tasty new shoots and leaves.

• One full carrier bag of nettles is roughly 1lb.

❦ NETTLES TO TICKLE YOUR FANCY MAN ❦

In Shetland, love-struck lassies used nettles to try to win over their man. At
Halloween, so the story goes, desperate maidens stole into the bedrooms of
their loved ones and placed nettles between the blankets. When the beau
went to sleep, he would be 'stung' by the magical properties of the nettles,
and 'stung' with love and desire for the maid.

NETTLES FOR YOUR HEALTH

Nettles are the staple of a traditional medicine cabinet and have long been known as a spring tonic, renowned for their ability to fortify, recharge and detoxify the sick, cold-ridden, and winter-weary. Nettles have high levels of vitamins A and C, and are a good tonic for blood.

Nettles are finally making a comeback from weed to superfood – rich in minerals such as calcium, magnesium, iron, and potassium. They have an unusual mineral profile, including manganese, which is a catalyst in the uptake of iron, setting a pattern of absorption, helping the body absorb iron and vitamins more easily.

Nettles and dandelions are also very good at detoxifying the liver, and young nettle and dandelion leaves can be drunk as springtime herbal infusions to rid the body of a winter's worth of build up of liver toxins from all those wild Christmas parties.

Herbalists prescribe nettles to relieve hay fever and allergies because of their anti-inflammatory properties. Nettles also relieve sufferers of other kinds of inflammation: gout, arthritis and rheumatism.

The Romans first introduced us to the nettle cure for rheumatism: their treatment involved alternating hot steam baths with a good self-flagellation with nettles. In true Presbyterian style, miners in Fife, Scotland, cut out the luxurious part of the treatment - the steam bath – and treated their rheumatic aches and pains after a day down the pit by simply thrashing their aching joints with nettles. The same method is still used among indigenous peoples in South America and New Guinea.

Eat nettles to get rid of stiff muscles after rigorous exercise, as they help eliminate toxins that build up in muscle tissue.

REAL MEN EAT NETTLES!

The long-running enmity between the Highlanders and Lowlanders of Scotland even stretched as far as what vegetables they ate. Not only was the weather soft in the Lowlands, so were the people, as seen by their taste in greens.

In the 18th century, the Lowlanders developed a taste for kale, while the Highlanders preferred the common nettle. The Highlanders regarded eating kale as a sign of effeminacy, labelling the Lowlanders 'Kale-eating-girlies'.

COOKING WITH NETTLES

NETTLE GNOCCHI WITH BLUE CHEESE SAUCE

Makes 6–8 servings.

The sight of a table-full of free greens cheers our Scottish hearts, as we mentally calculate the cost of 2lb of organic spinach from the supermarket.

Nettles have a wonderful smell and a sweet, delicate taste that is complemented by the salty blue cheese. We chose Cashel Blue cheese for this sauce, but any cheese will do. If you are feeding it to children, sell it as 'green mac and cheese' substituting a cheddar cheese sauce for the blue cheese. Alternatively, you could eat the gnocchi with a tomato-based sauce.

Make sure you use enough flour to stop the gnocchi sticking, otherwise your hands will end up looking like Shrek's. You don't need to be too precious about how the dumplings look: half the fun is playing with the dough balls and getting messy.

400g/1lb	NETTLES (about one full supermarket bag)
1.3kg/3lb	POTATOES, PEELED
2	EGGS
½ tsp	GRATED NUTMEG
	SEA SALT AND FRESHLY GROUND BLACK PEPPER
100–200g/3½–7oz	FLOUR
Knob	BUTTER

1. Prepere the nettles. There is no need to pick the nettle leaves from the stalks; at this time of year nettles are tender enough to eat whole. Put the gloves on, and put the nettles into a large pan of boiling water for 5–10 minutes. Then immediately drain and rinse the nettles under cold running water to cool as quickly as possible. Then squeeze all excess water out, and finely chop the nettles, either by hand or in a food processor.

2. Cook the potatoes in boiling water for about 15 minutes until tender, drain well then mash thoroughly until as smooth as possible.

3. Combine warm mashed potatoes, eggs, nutmeg, salt and pepper. Add the nettle mixture. Lightly mix together.

Add flour till dough comes together and shape into a big ball that is barely sticky on the outside.

Spring Nettles

4. Pick off balls of dough about an inch in diameter and, on a floured surface, roll them into small grub shaped lengths and pinch in the middle with a fork. Keep on a floured surface until all the gnocchi are made.

5. When ready to serve, plunge the gnocchi into plenty of boiling salted water. The gnocchi are cooked when they rise to the surface.

6. Strain and toss with butter.

BLUE CHEESE SAUCE *Makes 4–6 servings.*

200g/7oz CASHEL BLUE CHEESE, OR ANY OTHER BLUE CHEESE
30–60ml/1–2fl oz MILK

1. Melt the cheese in a saucepan, then mix in the milk until it is the consistency of white sauce.

NETTLE SOUP *Makes 6 servings.*

Whenever you mention cooking with nettles to anyone, they immediately say 'nettle soup'; it is the most traditional nettle dish, but it is also incredibly flavoursome, and simple to make. This holds up at a dinner party and with our children, who call it 'green soup' and lap it up like kittens.

This recipe also works with watercress (good with lemon juice added), or any other greens.

1 medium/large	ONION
450g/1lb	(4 medium-sized) POTATOES, PEELED
60g/2oz	BUTTER OR EXTRA-VIRGIN OLIVE OIL
275–300g/½–¾lb	NETTLES
1–1.5 litres/2–3 pints	GOOD CHICKEN STOCK
	NUTMEG, GRATED
	SEA SALT AND FRESHLY GROUND BLACK PEPPER
	SINGLE OR DOUBLE CREAM (OPTIONAL)

1. Chop the onion. Wash the potatoes and chop into small chunks (each potato into 4–6 pieces).

2. Heat the butter/olive oil in a large saucepan and soften the onion (about 5 minutes). Add the potatoes and cook for a couple of minutes more. Put to one side.

3. Wash the nettles, and blanch in boiling water for about a minute, then cool immediately by running under cold water.

4. Add the nettles to the saucepan with the onions and potatoes, then add the chicken stock so that it more than covers the ingredients by at least a third in volume.

5. Add some grated nutmeg and salt and pepper.

6. Cook for about 15 minutes until the potatoes are soft.

7. Liquidise the soup with a hand blender or in a food processor.

8. Adjust seasoning to taste.

9. Serve hot with a glob of cream, if desired.

NETTLE RISOTTO *Makes 4–6 servings.*

This is an Italian inspired recipe that works well; the creaminess of the rice and parmesan is offset nicely by the tender succulent leaves. The main secret of this dish is to make sure that the leaves are fresh and young.

600g/1lb 4oz	NETTLES (OR TRY A COMBINATION OF SPRING GREENS, INCLUDING SORREL, WILD GARLIC, DANDELION LEAVES)
2.2 litres/4 pints	GOOD CHICKEN STOCK
90ml/3fl oz	EXTRA-VIRGIN OLIVE OIL
1	ONION, FINELY CHOPPED
600g/1lb 4oz	ARBORIO RICE
150g/5oz	FRESHLY GRATED PARMESAN CHEESE
	SEA SALT AND FRESHLY GROUND BLACK PEPPER

1. If using just nettles, blanch in boiling water for about 1 minute, then immediately drain and rinse under cold running water to cool. Squeeze out the excess water.

2. Bring the stock to the boil in a saucepan and then simmer gently.

3. Heat the olive oil in a heavy saucepan over a low heat. Add the onion and nettles/ greens and fry gently, stirring continuously for about five minutes.

4. Add the rice and stir well, then cover with ladleful of warm stock so that it just covers the rice. Stir well. As rice absorbs the stock, stir in more liquid a ladleful at a time, never allowing the rice to become dry.

5. When the rice is cooked, after about fifteen minutes, remove the saucepan from the heat, stir in the parmesan and season to taste with salt and pepper.

6. Cover and leave to stand for a few minutes. The consistency should have movement without being runny. Serve immediately.

GOING GREEN

{ Chickweed, Dandelion Leaves, Goosegrass, Ground Elder, Hawthorn Leaves, Hedge Garlic, Sorrel, Watercress }

NETTLE ALOO *Makes 4–6 servings.*

450g/1lb POTATOES (about 4 mediu⌐
225g/8oz NETTLES
45g/2 tbsp BUTTER/OIL
1 tsp MUSTARD SEEDS
1 large ONION, SLICED
1–2 GARLIC GLOVES, PEELED AND C
1 tsp GROUND CORIANDER
1 tsp PAPRIKA
1 pinch CARDAMOM SEEDS
1 pinch CAYENNE PEPPER
SEA SALT AND FRESHLY GROUND BLAC⌐

1. Chop the potatoes into 3-centimetre (1-in⌐ place in a saucepan.

2. Wash the nettles and blanch in boiling water minute, drain, rinse under cold running water then squeeze the excess water out.

3. Combine potatoes and nettles in the saucepan. C⌐ with water and bring to the boil. Simmer for 10–12⌐ minutes, or until the potato pieces are just tender. D⌐ the potatoes and nettles thoroughly and put back into the pan.

4. In another pan, heat the butter or oil and cook the mustard seeds until they start to pop.

5. Add the onion and garlic and sauté until soft. Then add the spices.

6. Stir around then remove from the heat. Add the drained potato and nettles.

7. Stir gently, making sure the potato does not fall apart, and season to taste.

8. Return to the heat and simmer until most of the liquid has reduced.

SPRING GREENS

Date: *15 April 2007*
Weather: *Warm and sunny*
Place: *Riverbank, Central Edinburgh*
Objective: *Spring green salad*

An old friend, Kate, comes up from the Big Smoke to Edinburgh to forage with us. She's successful and single, always jetting off to exotic locations to do documentaries on NASA, or Egyptian mummies. Surely, our provincial tales of domestic drudgery and weed-picking can't hold much attraction to someone like her.

But I guess the grass is always greener. She arrives, excited about the prospect of a walk in the woods to pick enough greens for a spring green salad. We are slightly nervous that we won't live up to her expectations.

We decide to head for the riverbank just a short walk from my house, and we hope to prove that you don't have to be living in 'River Cottage' to enjoy the fruits of nature; that organic edibles are just minutes away from Princes Street.

We grab a few plastic supermarket bags, and shove them in our pockets, along with some gardening gloves and a pair of scissors. We're all set.

We show Kate how to identify Jack-by-the-hedge – also known as mustard garlic or hedge garlic – a tall upright plant with bright green leaves and small white flowers, which, when crushed, smells and tastes of garlic.

We stumble up a shady bank, far away from the well-trodden dog path, to pick a patch of chickweed. It is mild tasting, a bit like large cress.

Next, it's bishop's weed, goutweed or ground elder (**Aegopodium podagraria**), a voracious creeping weed, the bane of gardeners everywhere, but edible and, picked fresh, surprisingly tasty.

A few leaves of sweet cicely, identifiable by the sweet smell of liquorice and the white splodges on the leaves, can be added to salads or stewed fruit.

We're in the zone now, Kate's enthusiasm is growing by the minute, and a whole new world reveals itself. We find wood sorrel, its pretty delicate white flower next to its droopy shamrock-shaped leaves, growing under the trees.

Our salad bag is full, and we've only walked half a mile. We decide to head home and whip up our salad for lunch. We put all our ingredients in the salad spinner, wash the leaves, pick over them to remove any roots, and toss them in a large salad bowl with a honey vinaigrette. Grated pecorino on top, and a hunk of crusty bread with dollops of butter, we sit down over a bottle of Pinot Grigio, and catch up on 15 years of lost news.

SPRING GREEN SALAD

You don't have to be a purist; gather some wild greens and mix them in with your cultivated leaves. It's a great way of adding something really fresh to your salads while keeping your grocery bills down. A spring salad in March and April can consist of a variety of dandelion leaves and flowers, Jack-by-the-hedge, wild garlic leaves and flowers, hawthorn leaves, sorrel, wood sorrel, chickweed, ground elder, sweet cicely leaves, hairy bittercress, primrose flowers.

All spring greens are full of vitamins, and have long been eaten as a tonic after a long winter. They are best eaten in the spring before they flower: after that, the chemical content of the leaves changes, and they become bitter.

DANDELION
{*Taraxacum officinale*}

The dandelion is a ubiquitous weed related to the sunflower and chicory. In England, in the 19th century, it was grown in kitchen gardens and brought to market, some blanched like chicory. In France, today, dandelion leaves are still sold in markets in spring, the young leaves mixed in with other tender greens. Dandelion folk names include lion's tooth, bitterwort, wild endive, priest's crown, doonheadclock, piss-a-bed, Irish daisy, blow ball, puffball, clockflower, swine snout and cankerwort. In equal measures, it is loved by children  dandelion leaves

who like telling the time by it, and despaired at by gardeners who struggle with getting its root system out of their borders.

Since the 10th century, dandelion leaves, flowers and roots have been used as a mild laxative, safe diuretic, blood purifier, tonic and stimulant to the system. It is also believed to offer relief for rheumatism and arthritis. The dandelion contains more iron and calcium than spinach, and its leaves more vitamin A than carrots.

IDENTIFICATION

FIND IT HERE:
Lawns, parkland, fields.
WHAT IT LOOKS LIKE:
The leaves are roughly toothed,
growing from the base of the plant.
BEST TIME TO PICK:
February–April, before it flowers,
and use only the youngest leaves.

COMMONSENSE TIPS

• Pick the leaves before the dandelion flowers.

• If the leaves are not young enough, you can place a flowerpot or other container over the leaves to 'force' new young leaves through.

• Don't pick leaves out of grass that has lots of dog traffic

COOKING WITH DANDELIONS

GRANNY ISA'S DANDELION SALAD *Makes 6 servings.*

This recipe comes from a forager friend, Carolyn Rann, who learnt the tricks of the trade from her grandmother.

2 large **POTATOES**
1 medium **ONION, FINELY CHOPPED**
6 slices **STREAKY BACON OR SPECK, CUT INTO SMALL PIECES**
2 tbsp **EXTRA-VIRGIN OLIVE OIL**
2 large bunches **YOUNG DANDELION LEAVES**
1 tbsp **WHITE-WINE VINEGAR**
6 **EGGS**

1. Boil the potatoes, drain (reserving the water) and slice up, then mix with the chopped onion.

2. Fry the bacon or speck in the olive oil until crispy, then add to the potato-and-onion mixture.

3. Put the washed dandelion leaves into the bowl.

4. Heat up the vinegar, which can be diluted with some of the reserved cooking liquid from the potatoes.

5. Pour over the potatoes and season with salt and freshly ground black pepper and toss.

6. Serve with runny poached eggs allowing one egg per person.

JACK-BY-THE-HEDGE
{Alliaria petiolata}

Jack-by-the-hedge, also known as hedge garlic or mustard garlic, doesn't have as strong a flavour or smell as wild garlic, so it is good to use if you want to add a subtle flavouring of garlic to a dish or salad but don't want the taste and smell of garlic to overpower. Its numerous names are, per-haps, an indication of its ubiquity, as it grows everywhere.

IDENTIFICATION

FIND IT HERE:
Hedgerows, roadsides, open woodland.
BEST TIME TO PICK:
February–April, before it flowers. Some-times produces a flowerless second crop in the autumn.
WHAT IT LOOKS LIKE:
The leaves are bright green, large, but thin, ivy-shaped, with small-toothed edges, and are hairy underneath. The flowers are small and white. The plant tends to be tall and leggy, with a straight stalk, and can grow to 70 centimetres (28 inches) tall.

COMMONSENSE TIPS

• Try to pick the youngest greenest leaves before it flowers.

COOKING WITH HEDGE GARLIC

Hedge garlic is an excellent salad plant and makes a good addition to sauces for fish, giving a mild garlicky flavour. Remember to add the leaves at the end of cooking for maximum flavour.

HEDGE GARLIC SAUCE FOR LAMB

2 handfuls **HEDGE-GARLIC LEAVES, FINELY CHOPPED**
2 tbsp **VINEGAR**
SUGAR TO TASTE
1 **TORN-UP MINT LEAF**

1. Wash and dry the hedge-garlic leaves, chop finely and add the vinegar.

2. Add the sugar by teaspoons until the right sweetness.

3. Add the mint leaf for an extra taste sensation.

CHICKWEED
{*Stellaria media*}

Chickweed is that plant that grows in your planter or window box when you haven't tended it for a while. Rich in phosphorous, potassium and iron, it is worth slipping the young shoots into your spring list of ingredients.

This weed is a common ingredient in all sorts of skin creams, as it is a very good salve for sensitive or irritated skin.

IDENTIFICATION

FIND IT HERE:
Chickweed is a very common herb that grows on disused ground. It grows along road/path sides and creeps into unkempt places such as old window boxes or cracks in the pavement. It grows throughout the year.

WHAT IT LOOKS LIKE:
The plant grows in an untidy-carpet pattern. The small white star-shaped flowers make the plant easily identifiable.

WHAT CAN IT BE CONFUSED WITH?:
The only plant you are likely to confuse chickweed with is the smaller, sparser-leaved mouse-ear chickweed. This chickweed isn't poisonous, it just tastes disgusting, and is therefore inedible.

- The bright green stems and oval leaves can be cooked as a vegetable, and, if picked early enough in the season, taste like tender baby spinach.

- It is easier to pick if you have scissors.

Commonsense tips.

COOKING WITH CHICKWEED

Think cress, think chickweed; that is exactly how we have been using it. It is crunchy in sandwiches, the kids munch it up squeezed in alongside egg, marmite, tuna, chicken, cream cheese or ham. It smells good while it is cooking, and tastes delicious raw in salads and sandwiches. Chickweed can be used like spinach or as an addition to stews, soups and sauces.

CHICKWEED SANDWICH MIX

1 bunch CHICKWEED
LEMON JUICE
WORCESTERSHIRE SAUCE
SEA SALT AND FRESHLY GROUND BLACK PEPPER

1. To the chickweed, add a little bit of lemon juice, a few drops of Worcestershire sauce and salt and pepper, to taste.

2. To make a sandwich, combine the chickweed mixture with chicken, ham, tomatoes, peanut butter etc.

GROUND ELDER
{*Aegopodium podograria*}

Brought over by the Romans as a potherb, this is probably the most perni-
cious and, therefore, hated garden weed. The good news is that you can eat
it, provided the leaves are young and glossy. It has an interesting aromatic
taste and is a good source of iron.

IDENTIFICATION

FIND IT HERE:
Gardens, hedgerows, woodlands, waste ground.
BEST TIME TO PICK:
April to June.

find it here.

WHAT IS LOOKS LIKE:
Trifoliate leaves which are pointed and irregularly toothed. It is a low growing plant, but spreads upwards to a metre tall. White florets, comprising 10
to 20 umbels, are carried on a tall, hollow stem.

COMMONSENSE TIPS

* Can be cooked and used like spinach.

SORREL
{*Rumex acetosa*}

Date: *May 2007*
Place: *Fife Woodland*
Objective: *A walk in the woods*

We get down on our hands and knees and start scouring the grass for
sorrel's distinctive, arrow-shaped leaf. It's late May, so it's easier to find
– the long stalks with the reddish tiny balls of flower have started to poke
up through the long grass.

  We find a choice leaf and hand it to Claire to try. She looks at us as if
we're barmy, but takes a bite anyway. It takes a while for the lemony tang
in sorrel to come through. She munches for a while, not saying anything,
then suddenly her eyes narrow.

'It's like toxic waste!' she announces. We're not sure whether to feel offended or worried. She explains that 'toxic waste' is a children's boiled sweet, which like sorrel, only hits you with a bang after a few seconds in your mouth.

'It's got a nice aftertaste,' she says, so we decide to give some to Charlie, aged four.

'It's yummy,' he declares.

Soon the news travels, and the three girls crowd round. They all taste it and very quickly we are trying to satisfy an insatiable demand from all four children for sorrel leaves. They just can't get enough of them, so we show them what to look for, and soon they are picking for themselves.

Later on, back home, Adair asks if he can have some sorrel in his schoolbag for snack. Now that beats Walker's crisps.

IDENTIFICATION

FIND IT HERE:
Sorrel grows in uncultivated grass and pasture, and can be picked as early as February. It goes on growing all year.

WHAT IT LOOKS LIKE:
A bit like dock (it is of the same *Rumex* family) but the leaf is distinctive in that it is usually smaller and is shaped like an arrowhead. Dock leaves are edible; eating dock leaves is supposed to have cured Julius Caesar's soldiers of scurvy! In summer, tall flowering stems appear, that can grow to between 60 centimetres (2 feet) and 1.2 metres (4 feet). The flowers appear as small, reddish-green balls.

There are three types of sorrel, and *Rumex acetosa* is the most common. French sorrel, *Rumex scutatus*, grows in mats, and the leaves can look like hearts as well as arrows. Sheep's sorrel, *Rumex acetosella*, grows in abundance on dry and acid soils. All three types are edible, and all have the tangy lemony taste.

Wood sorrel (*Oxalis acetosella*) is less common, as it grows mostly in ancient deciduous woods. It is a delicate-looking low creeping plant, with a leaf that looks like a shamrock, and small white flowers that come out in spring. Wood sorrel is less acid than the field sorrels, but can be used in the same way as them. In addition, the crushed leaves can be mixed with sugar and bottled to make 'lemonade' cordial.

*Sorrel
Spring Greens
Kettle*

FACT AND FOLKLORE:

• The name 'sorrel' comes from the old French '*surele*', meaning 'sour'.

• Sorrel is known as 'souroch' in Scotland for its sour taste.

• Traditionally, sorrel has been used in the home to remove stains from linen.

• Sorrel can be used in the dyeing process as both a colour brightener, and as a mordant. A mordant is used to stop the dyes from running.

• Sorrel is a thirst quencher and makes a refreshing tea. Scottish islanders on South Uist took an old kettle-full of water up on to the grazing ground with their cattle, and fired up a pot of tea using sorrel leaves to quench their thirsts.

COMMONSENSE TIPS

• Sorrel contains oxalic acid, which is what gives it its sour taste, and is toxic in excess as it encourages the formation of kidney stones, so don't overuse.

COOKING WITH SORREL

Sorrel gives off a sharp lemony taste to any dish, and a few sorrel leaves are an interesting addition to a green salad. The leaves tend to lose their tangy flavour if cooked for too long, so only add them towards the end of cooking. Don't cook anything containing sorrel in a nonstick or iron pan – the acid in the leaves will react and take on a metallic taste.

We have used sorrel as an interesting addition to all sorts of dishes. It can be mixed with breadcrumbs, egg yolks and butter, and used as a stuffing for fish. Alternatively, you can chop the leaves and add them to melted butter, and use this sauce to pour over fish or potatoes.

SAUCY SORREL

Every gourmet deli these days sells sorrel sauce at vast expense in little jars, but sorrel sauce can be as easy to make as white sauce, adding the sorrel leaves at the end of cooking.

Sorrel sauce is delicious over white fish, scallops or even baked ham. Also, try adding sorrel leaves to to mayonnaise or mashed potatoes.

SORREL SAUCE HOLLANDAISE *Makes 4–6 servings.*

This is a hollandaise-type sauce that works well with any poached fish, or for a sorrel-inspired eggs Benedict. Make sure you don't get overzealous when adding the butter to the eggs, otherwise this can be the most frustrating cooking experience as you watch your creation curdle and you have to start all over again.

125g/4oz SORREL LEAVES
2 SHALLOTS (or 2 heaped tbsp ONION), CHOPPED
2 tbsp VERMOUTH, MADEIRA OR SHERRY
4 tbsp DRY WHITE WINE
4 tbsp WATER
3 large EGG YOLKS
225g/8oz LIGHTLY SALTED BUTTER

1. Wash the sorrel leaves and cut them into small strips.

2. Combine the shallots or onions with the wines and water, and boil gently until the liquid has reduced and the onions are barely covered.

3. Put the onions and the egg yolks in a blender and mix for about 30 seconds.

4. Melt the butter in a pan with half the sorrel leaves.

5. When the butter has melted, remove from the heat and pour on to the egg yolks very gradually, stirring vigorously, otherwise the mixture will curdle. The speed can be increased once the sauce thickens.

6. Season, to taste, and gradually add the rest of the sorrel leaves.

7. If reheating the sauce, do so over a gentle heat or a bain-marie, otherwise it will curdle.

SPRING GREEN TEMPURA *Makes 4 servings.*

All sorts of spring green leaves can be dipped in batter and cooked in hot oil, drained and served. It's simple, easy and fun. The best leaves to use are 'substantial' leaves, such as bistort, ground elder, nettles, sorrel and wild garlic, or a herb that you might have in your garden, such as sage.

There's no need for deep-fat fryers for this recipe: simply put a couple of inches of light oil (such as sunflower oil) in a pan and heat it up until it is smoking. We have used a tempura batter recipe, which uses cold water instead of milk for the batter – it gives the tempura a much lighter texture. Don't make the batter ahead of time, and don't overmix it.

To check the temperature of the frying oil, drop a little batter into the oil. If the batter comes up right away instead of sinking to the bottom of the pan, it's about the right temperature.

A COUPLE OF HANDFULS OF SPRING LEAVES SUCH AS SORREL, WILD GARLIC, SAGE, NETTLE, YOUNG DANDELION, HEDGE GARLIC

FOR THE TEMPURA BATTER:

1 EGG
250ml/8 fl oz ICE-COLD WATER
150g/5oz PLAIN FLOUR
VEGETABLE OIL FOR DEEP FRYING

1. Make the batter immediately before use. Beat the egg and add the iced water. This prevents the batter from absorbing too much oil, keeping it light and crispy.

2. Lightly mix in the flour with a fork and beat gently. Don't worry about lumps.

3. Dip the leaves and greens in the batter, allowing it to coat them thoroughly.

4. Heat the vegetable oil in a deep pan. If the coated greens sink to the bottom of the pan the temperature is too high.

KOREAN DIPPING SAUCE

1 small CLOVE OF GARLIC, CRUSHED
1 SPRING ONION, CHOPPED
4 tbsp SOY SAUCE

2 tbsp **WHITE VINEGAR (OR WINE VINEGAR)**
1 tbsp **SESAME OIL**
1 tsp **SUGAR**
1 tsp **ROASTED SESAME SEEDS (OPTIONAL)**
¼ tsp **CHILLI POWDER (OPTIONAL)**

1. Combine all the ingredients in a bowl and mix. If you don't have these specialised ingredients to hand, simply combine soy sauce, sugar, and some balsamic vinegar, and a dash of anything you fancy, such as Tabasco or chilli sauce.

SORREL AND CUCUMBER SOUP *Makes 6 servings.*

Good handful **SORREL LEAVES, RINSED AND PICKED OVER, TORN UP, STEMS DISCARDED**
1 thin **CUCUMBER, CHOPPED**
2 fat **SPRING ONIONS**
1 **GARLIC CLOVE, SLICED**
1.1 litres/2 pints **CHICKEN STOCK**
150ml/5½fl oz **CARTON OF SINGLE CREAM**
SEA SALT AND FRESHLY GROUND BLACK PEPPER

1. Place the sorrel leaves, cucumber, spring onions, garlic and chicken stock into a pan and simmer until the cucumber and spring onions are soft.
2. Allow the mixture to cool and then purée with a blender.
3. Pour in the single cream, stir well and season to taste.
4. Chill the soup for at least an hour.
5. Serve cold, in small bowls.

HAWTHORN

{Crataegus monogyna}

Hawthorn, otherwise known as 'May', is one of the most stunning shrubs to adorn our hedgerows in the spring when it is blossoming. The flowers (mayflowers) can be made into wine in the spring, and the berries (haws) are made into jellies and wine in the autumn.

IDENTIFICATION

FIND IT HERE:
Hawthorn grows up to eight metres high, and is the most common shrub growing in our hedgerows, woodlands and scrublands. The creamy-pink flowers appear between April and June, and are pollinated by flies, not bees.

WHAT IT LOOKS LIKE:
The leaves are small and glossy green and grow on spiny branches, and are the first leaves to come out in spring. Hawthorn produces one of the earliest blossoms in spring.

COMMONSENSE TIPS

• Picked, and chopped roughly, new young shoots make a laudable alternative to flat-leafed parsley.

HAWTHORN TABBOULEH

125g/4oz CRACKED WHEAT
Juice 3 LEMONS
75ml/3fl oz EXTRA-VIRGIN OLIVE OIL
1 handful NEW HAWTHORN LEAVES, FINELY CHOPPED
3 RIPE TOMATOES, FINELY CHOPPED
1 medium RED ONION, FINELY SLICED
1 large bunch MINT
SEA SALT AND FRESHLY GROUND BLACK PEPPER

1. Soak the cracked wheat in cold water for 20 minutes, then rinse and drain, squeezing out any excess water.

2. Place in a bowl, add lemon juice, and leave to soak for 10 minutes before adding the olive oil.

3. Add the hawthorn leaves, tomatoes and onion and mix thoroughly.

4. Add salt and pepper, to taste.

LIVING OFF THE LAND

I had seen a picture of Rosalind Burgess on the back of her wild-food cookbook, **Island Kitchen**, where she is kneeling shyly on a picnic rug that is anchored down by quiches, pastries and home-made wine. It looked unquestionably 70s to me, with the white cheesecloth shirt, striped skirt and braid dropping straight down her back. As I was in Skye, anyway, I decided to pay her a visit.

Simon drops me off at the gate, to go and test the local ale in the Steine Arms, while I watch a figure in the distance push a wheelbarrow round the corner of her storybook white-washed cottage. I don't want to shout in case I scare her. She pushes the empty barrow towards me, and smiles as she beckons for me to come and sit down on a rickety deckchair. She is living the good life, I observe, as I take in her neat garden with its rows of leeks and strawberries.

Rosalind arrived on the island as a young woman, thirty years ago, with no money and a boyfriend who then returned to the mainland on his own. She started collecting whelks, winkles, razor fish and mussels off the beach because she was broke, then sold her beach forage for cash. The locals taught her how to collect wild edibles, as they had done as children.

The strangest dish she has ever cooked? 'Hawthorn Dumplings; I ate them with chopped liver and bacon. Everyone said they were delicious.'

Now she forages for flowers and plants to dye wool with. 'Come into the house and see some examples of my work,' she urges.

I follow her into a tiny hall that opens up into a small but immaculate kitchen. A rocking chair sits idle in front of a blue enamel range with highly polished lids, knitting sits next to the chair.

'It keeps me busy in the evening,' she says, seeing me glance at her handiwork. A spinning wheel stands to the right of the cooker, everything neat as a pin. In her front room is the loom taking up half the space; behind it hang reams of wool, which she dyes herself. The lichens and tansy produce ochres and browns, and she also uses meadowsweet and bog myrtle. 'I do buy some dyes in,' she reveals.

Simon returns from the pub, having set the car alarm off and creating more irritation in ten minutes than Rosalind, no doubt, in all her years in the neighbourhood. Her world – where no one is in a hurry – is suddenly very compelling, with the view, the smell of salt and bog myrtle in the air and the mewl of the gulls wheeling over her head.

We drive away, leaving her waving at the gate. I think how good she is at the survival game, although, no doubt, Rosalind would never see it like that.

ROSALIND'S GROUND ELDER AND CHICKPEA SALAD *Makes 4 servings.*

225g/8oz	**CHICKPEAS**
Good handful	**OF GROUND ELDER OR YOUNG HAWTHORN LEAVES**
150ml/¼ pint	**NATURAL YOGHURT**
½tsp	**GROUND CORIANDER**
½tsp	**GROUND CUMIN**
1tsp	**FRESHLY CHOPPED SAGE**
1 clove	**GARLIC**
juice ½	**LEMON**
	FRESHLY GROUND PEPPER

1. Soak the beans overnight, strain and simmer gently in a saucepan of fresh water for about an hour. Drain and allow to cool.

2. Finely chop the leaves, mix the yoghurt and the spices, sage, garlic, lemon juice and pepper, and combine all ingredients.

GOOSEGRASS

{*Galium aparine*}

We know, this is an unusual one to be thinking of eating. We usually associate sticky willy, goosegrass or cleavers with the childhood joke of sneaking up and sticking it to an adult's back, or pulling it out of the garden. But it has an altogether higher purpose: this herb strengthens your immune system and metabolism as well as having diuretic and laxative effects.

IDENTIFICATION

FIND IT HERE:
Anywhere – gardens, woodlands, hedgerows, fields, parks.

WHAT IT LOOKS LIKE:
A straggling, bristly annual that has 'sticky' bristles that attach to other plants and clothing.

COMMONSENSE TIPS

- Try to pick young, bright green specimens, before the sticky balls form.

- Pick away from high traffic areas.

goosegrass and vegetable

SWAMP JUICE

Our kids loved making this juice, and they liked the taste. We suggest putting the goosegrass in the juicer first – the liquid comes out the colour of wheatgrass and ends up an interesting colour when you mix in the other vegetables.

2	RIPE TOMATOES
2 sticks	CELERY
1	CARROT
1 bunch	YOUNG GOOSEGRASS
1 pinch	SEA SALT
	SQUEEZE LEMON JUICE

1. Put the goosegrass in the juicer first, add all the other ingredients, then mix.

WATERCRESS
{*Roripa nasturtiun-aquaticum*}

Watercress has been given great press recently as a 'superfood', and, certainly, the strong, peppery taste is very satisfying. The fear of the water-borne parasite 'liver fluke' puts many people off eating wild watercress, but, if cooked, it is safe to eat.

IDENTIFICATION

FIND IT HERE:
In any river, stream or ditch, where there is running water, throughout Britain, except in the Highlands and northern Wales, from April to October.

WHAT IT LOOKS LIKE:
Silky green leaves, with small white flower blossoms between May and October.

COMMONSENSE TIPS

• Don't pick in stagnant water.

• Pick the older, darker leaves, as they have more taste.

• Wash well before cooking.

• Wild watercress should only be eaten raw if you are certain that no sheep or cattle have been drinking from the water or grazing upstream from where you are picking.

WATERCRESS SOUP

To make a delicious watercress soup, simply follow the recipe for Nettle Soup (Page 23), substituting watercress for the nettles, and adding a squeeze of lemon. It can also be served cold, with ground almonds and the juice and zest of an orange and some single cream.

SMOKED MACKEREL AND WATERCRESS PIE

Makes 6 servings.

6 handfuls	WATERCRESS
800g–1kg/2lb	WAXY NEW POTATOES
500g/1lb	SMOKED MACKEREL
10 fl oz	DOUBLE CREAM
4 fl oz	WHOLE MILK
3 tbsp	HORSERADISH

1. Blanch the watercress, and chop roughly.

2. Slice the potatoes to about the thickness of a £1 coin, and steam until just tender.

3. Flake the smoked mackerel into an ovenproof dish, and spread the watercress over the fish.

4. Combine the cream, milk and horseradish, and pour over the top of the fish and watercress.

5. Layer potatoes on top, and bake in a preheated oven (225°F/110°C/Gas ¼) for 40 minutes. Serve with grilled tomatoes and broad beans.

WATERCRESS MINESTRONE *Makes 8 servings.*

2 small	RED ONIONS
2 cloves	GARLIC
1	CELERY HEART
3 tbsp	EXTRA-VIRGIN OLIVE OIL
500g/1lb	WATERCRESS
500g/1lb	GREEN BEANS
2 x 235g/8oz cans	CANNELLINI BEANS
250g /½lb	PEAS (FRESH OR FROZEN)
750ml/1.3 pints	CHICKEN STOCK
	SEA SALT AND FRESHLY GROUND BLACK PEPPER
½ bunch	MINT
300ml/10fl oz	DOUBLE CREAM
100g/3.5oz	PARMESAN CHEESE, FRESHLY GRATED

1. Peel and chop the onions, garlic and celery, and fry gently in the olive oil for 10 minutes.

2. Wash the watercress thoroughly, then chop, and cut the green beans into 3-centimetre (1-inch) pieces.

3. Drain the cannellini beans.

4. Add half of the watercress, green beans and peas to the onion mixture, and cook for 10 minutes.

5. Add the stock, season with salt and pepper, then add the cannellini beans and the remaining watercress, green beans and peas.

6. Cook for 10 minutes more, and then add the mint, cream and Parmesan.

7. Allow to cool slightly and serve.

EASTER PUDDING – OH, HOW OUR TASTES HAVE REFINED!

Date: *March 2007*

Place: *Lammermuirs*

Objective: *Hedgerow history revealed*

It's springtime, and we are out for a walk with botanist Dr Brian Moffat. We are walking down a hillside lane, and the views across East Lothian and Edinburgh to the north are stunning. We are talking plants, and he tells us of growing up in Cumbria. Every Easter, his family prepare a Cumberland pudding (or Easter pudding), using young bistort and sweet cicely leaves, and other spring-green edibles from the hedgerow. We are intrigued. We have read about Easter pudding, but never eaten it.

'You have to adjust the recipe, depending on your tastes. Cicely is very aniseed, bistort is very strong, they don't really go. Young nettles went in,' he says with considerable pride.

1. Cloth laid

'It sounds pretty unpalatable,' we tell him, making a mental note not to accept invitations to tea at his house.

'Well, I like it, but, me, I eat spinach substitutes whenever I can get them,' Moffat says with no trace of irony.

2. Pudding Packed in

'It's only to be eaten on Easter Sunday. The leaves are in bulk then, they are worth gathering,' Moffat says, sounding defensive, it is his home patch after all.

It was originally an Easter dish, when watercress and bistort (also known as Easterman giants, or Easter ledges) could be included.

Some of the Cumbrian pride in bistort could come from the fact that it is not native to Scotland; bistort stops at Gretna. Moffat talks of people north of the Border having planted it, purely for its great healing and medicinal powers. 'In those days, they ate food because it was good for them, not because it tasted nice,' Moffat tells us. Point taken.

3. Cloth Knotted

In Cumbria, there were competitions to see who could make the best Easter pudding. It was also considered a fertility pudding, traditionally eaten in the last two weeks of Lent by women who were trying to conceive. Worth a try, we think, if we were in the market for a baby; beats IVF.

We decide to follow a traditional 1950s Cumbrian Women's Institute recipe, (passed on by a botanist, Professor Mary Gibbs), so we can go some way to understanding what all the fuss is about.

The conclusion? Tastes have changed since the 1950s. We manage a slice but we can't get the children to touch it. Admittedly, the cabbage has turned khaki and the alchemilla leaf, a staple of mediaeval kitchens and which we decided to put in at the last minute, was, perhaps, a tad too adventurous for our modern palate; it turned an unappealing dark sludgy brown. Unappetising to look at, uninspiring in taste. Or perhaps we just failed the WI Easter Pudding Competition. We vowed to recreate a modern version of the same recipe, and take it to Cumbria next spring.

🏃 EASTER LUNCH 🏃

Nettle Soup

*

Granny Isa's Dandelion Salad

*

Chicken stuffed with Wild Garlic
Roast Potatoes with Spring Herbs

*

Blackcurrant Leaf Sorbet

🏃 KIDS' SPRING TEA 🏃

Spring Greens Soup

*

Chickweed and Marmite Sandwiches

*

Dyed Boiled Eggs

*

Crab Apple Syrup Muffins

🏃 KIDS' EASTER LUNCH 🏃

Nettle Gnocchi with Blue Cheese
Sauce

*

Vanilla Pudding with Rosehip Syrup

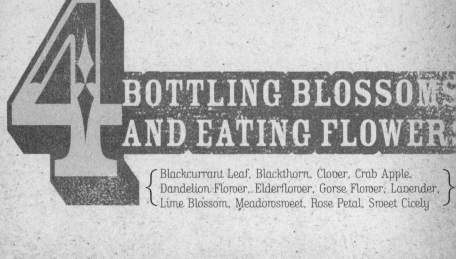

4

BOTTLING BLOSSOM AND EATING FLOWER

{ Blackcurrant Leaf, Blackthorn, Clover, Crab Apple,
Dandelion Flower, Elderflower, Gorse Flower, Lavender,
Lime Blossom, Meadowsweet, Rose Petal, Sweet Cicely }

EDIBLE BLOSSOMS

Date: *20 April 2007*
Place: *Communal gardens*
Objective: *Blossoms we can make into cordial*

'Lift me up, now!' Mungo shouts, as we haul him on to my shoulders so he can push his face into a drift of sweet-looking hawthorn blossom.

'Gross! This smells of nappies!' he says as we put him down on the ground with a jolt. We explain that it's because flies fertilise the hawthorn tree not bees, so it has to smell that way to attract the flies. We stop holding our noses, and decide to try the crab-apple tree down the bottom of the hill. Anyway, we've heard it's unlucky to bring hawthorn into the house, probably because it contains the same chemical, trimethylamine, as dead bodies. Just shows, there is logic behind some of these folklores.

We sniff a spray of white that is hanging down from a gnarled old tree. It smells of apples.

Lorne and Adair jump up and down to grab the lowest branches, pulling them down to bury their faces in blossom. 'Hey, it really does smell of apples, cool!' Adair says. The smell of wet nappies is long forgotten, as we start collecting crab-apple blossom to make cordial.

Lyn, the local gardener, walks past and wonders what we are doing squinting up into the tree. 'Got your Frisbee stuck, have you?' she asks.

'May we take a few branches off it?' we enquire. 'We want to pick blossom while the sun is shining and the petals are dry.'

'No problem, it could do with a prune.' Lyn replies – so far she has been very supportive off our cooking adventures. 'Just make sure it's not the bird cherry. George with the Border terrier told me that it's got cyanide in it.'

All the stone fruits, such as plums, peaches, apricots and cherries, have traces of cyanide in the stones, not the fruit, leaves or blossoms; but bird cherry is the only stone fruit where cyanide has been found in the fruit as well, but only when the fruit is aged. Cattle have died from eating bird-cherry leaves, and, though there is no record of any harm coming to anyone making cordial from the blossom, we've decided to steer clear.

'You say we are going to make juice out of this?' Lorne says, looking into our bag of blossom. 'How can you make a drink out of flowers? I mean, that's really dumb.'

We go home to prove him wrong.

BOTTLING BLOSSOM

You don't have to wait for elderflowers in May and June to make cordial. We spent an entire weekend in April walking in orchards and hedgerows, doing the smell check. We had cordials in mind; scented, aromatic, sweet concoctions that come as the harbinger of summer. In deciding what type of cordials to make, let your nose be the guide. That is the fun of it. It is the perfume that you are bottling. Some of the more showy sprays of flowers, such as cherries, the light pink and the dark pink, look great but do not really have a perfume at all, unlike the more heady fragrance of the lowly blackthorn and the delicate crisp aroma of the crab apple.

- You'll need a picking stick to pull the branches down. Use a shepherd's crook, or a walking stick, or make a picking stick by placing the top of a wire coat hanger into the top of a bamboo cane.

commonsense tips.
- Don't pick by a main road or similar polluted area. Roadsides and verges are often sprayed with weed killers.

- If you pick on the edge of fields, make sure you know whether the local farmer uses pesticides. Brown, curling, withered leaves are often an indication of pesticide use.

- The food you have harvested should be processed and eaten as soon as possible to pre-empt the fermentation process – put your hand into a bag of blossoms even as little as an hour after picking them and you will feel the heat building up.

- Best to pick into a bucket, as the flowers need air around them, otherwise mould can develop.

- Pick blossom sparingly; remember, the flowers produce the seed and, therefore, the fruit. Don't pick more than you can use in one session.

- Try not to crush the blossoms and leave a good amount of stalk and leaf behind. Handle carefully to avoid further decomposition.

- Pick when the sun is out; that is when the plants are at their best, as the sun stimulates the flow of nectar to the flower.

EARLY SPRING BLOSSOMS
BLACKTHORN
{Prunus spinosa}

Blackthorn is the first blossom of spring, found in April. We found that the sweet-smelling flowers made a delicious cordial, but we suggest that, if you do pick a bucket-load, you leave them outside the back door, until you need them, since some old wives' tales say that it is bad luck to have sprays of flowers in the house.

IDENTIFICATION

FIND IT HERE:
Found commonly in hedgerows, this shrub is unusual in that the flowers show – in April – before the leaves break out.

WHAT IT LOOKS LIKE:
White blossoms on a spiky branch. The berries of the blackthorn are the blue-black sloes, which are ready to pick in September/October.

WHAT IT CAN BE CONFUSED WITH:
Hawthorn is the next blossom to show – in May, hence, also called mayflowers – but, unlike blackthorn, the hawthorn leaves break out before the blossom. So, if it has blossom but no leaf, it is blackthorn. Let your nose be your guide: hawthorn smells vaguely of dead meat and is pollinated by flies, whereas blackthorn is sweetly perfumed.

CRAB APPLE
{Malus sylvestris}

Crab apple is the wild apple stock on which all cultivated apples are grown and from which they have been developed. Many of the so-called apple trees that we see in our hedgerows have come about through cultivated apple seeds that have been thrown out of the car window, or been brought by birds. Of all the blossoms this is one of the more sweetly scented, with just a hint of apples.

IDENTIFICATION

FIND IT HERE:
In people's gardens, orchards or in the hedgerows, in April and May.

WHAT IT LOOKS LIKE:
Small, deciduous, with small oval leaves and dark brown twigs. The flowers are pink and white with yellow stamens, and grow in clusters.

A SWEET DISTRACTION

Date: *3 May, Scottish Election day*
Place: *Riverbank*
Objective: *Past caring*

It's 3 May, Scottish Election day, and it's hot. Fiona is wearing a big rosette and a strained look on her face. We are under instructions not to discuss politics: 'The great thing is, it's too late to do any more anyway,' she says, wearily. Our walk along the Water of Leith in Edinburgh is a much-needed distraction. The kids are babbling away, pleased that the only kind of leaflets they are handling are green and bio-degradable, that they don't have to doorstep strangers, and that there isn't a letterbox in sight.

A woman with a retriever on a lead glares at our children as they dip off the path and proceed to slide down a muddy bank on their bottoms, screaming as they go. 'Oi, careful, you've only got one pair of school trousers,' I remind my son. It is then that I see our prize nestling in a large clump at the bottom of the bank in the long grass, shaded by the banks of the river. Sweet cicely (**Myrrhis odorata**) is a long-ago garden escapee, worth searching long and hard for – though it is easily found when you know the identification points – on roadside verges and shady wooded places.

After a thorough inspection – to check that the feathery leaves have patches of white (a little like flour) and smell of aniseed when rubbed, and that the creamy flat heads are heavily perfumed – we allow the kids to test for themselves. Lydia, aged nine, starts nibbling on the stem just below the flower head. 'It tastes of liquorice!' she says, her eyebrows arching, as if to say, Why didn't you tell me before?

'I don't like liquorice, do I, Mum?' Mungo declares, spitting his stalk out.

While we are picking the heads for cordial, Isobel, Mungo's cousin, scrapes her knee on a rock, having slid too fast down the bank. Her flimsy cotton dress is now dusty red.

'Wilderness first aid to the rescue.' Fiona heads off to find a plantain leaf (never far away), known as nature's band-aid, and a large dock leaf to wrap round her leg.

'They're huge!' cries Mungo, staring approvingly at the clump of giant dock leaves the size of jackrabbits' ears.

Isobel stops crying. The surprise at her wounds being treated with leaves is enough to make her feel better. Fiona is starting to look more relaxed: making a six-year-old's day by sucking a stalk and rubbing a leaf into a scratch, puts everything in perspective. Win or lose, this is what it's all really about.

SWEET CICELY
{*Myrrhis odorata*}

This ancient potherb escapee is a veritable gift to people who like interesting tasting leaves in their salads. This is a commonly found plant that is worth spotting and using in your cooking or including in a fruit smoothie for added sweetness at no calorific cost.

IDENTIFICATION

FIND IT HERE:
Sweet cicely is found in damp grassy habitats and waysides.

WHAT IT LOOKS LIKE:
This plant grows up to a metre or more high and is characterised by flat
creamy clusters of flowers and bright green feathery leaves that are smat-
tered with white spots. It flowers between April and June. In June and July,
it is characterised by gherkin-shaped pods that ripen to a dark brown.

WHAT IT CAN BE CONFUSED WITH:
At a quick glance, you could confuse it with a member of the cow parsley
umbellifers – the main differences are that the smell of the sweet cicely
blossom is a strong aniseed aroma, and the leaves, when pressed, also
smell of liquorice. The mottled white leaves are another good way to tell
this plant apart. This plant grows taller than cow parsley.

SWEET AS SUGAR, BUT NO CALORIES

Coca-Cola and PepsiCo are studying the properties of sweet cicely in the
hope that it will be the new sweetener for diet drinks, because it can taste
up to 800 times sweeter than cane sugar, but has none of the calories.

This is due to a chemical compound called 'trans-anethole', named after
the Latin name for aniseed *anitum*, which multiplies the sweetness of the
plant. If you break off the stem of sweet cicely and chew it, you get an over-
whelming sweet-liquorice taste. This is due to the trans-anethole, a taste
shared by several other plants, such as fennel and dill, and wild flowers,
such as restharrow.

Commonsense tips.

- The stalks taste like liquorice, and children love
sucking on them – nature's free sugar drip!

- Use the leaves chopped up and added to salads, or
stewed fruit such as gooseberries and rhubarb, or a
plate of strawberries, where it helps reduce the acidity.
This way, you will cut down on the amount of sugar that you need.

- You can boil or butter the roots and eat like parsnips.

- Infuse the whole plant in boiling water to make a herbal tea.

- The green seed pods, when gathered in June, are known as 'Scotch com-
fits', and have a nectar that tastes like a liquorice liquor.

MEADOWSWEET

{Filipendula ulmaria}

Meadowsweet, with its creamy-white heads, adorns riverside meadows in the summertime. Meadowsweet is an interesting medicinal plant, having been used for centuries as a fever reducer. It is used as a flavouring agent in traditional ales, and makes a great cordial with gooseberries.

Try making a meadowsweet cordial and using it to mix with other flavours.

A cordial of meadowsweet and elderflower is good – the meadowsweet taming the sweetness of the elderflower.

A glug of meadowsweet cordial in gooseberry fool, or other fruit desserts, adds an interesting flavour.

IDENTIFICATION

FIND IT HERE:
Meadowsweet likes its feet wet. Ubiquitous anywhere damp, such as riverbanks and boggy ground.

WHAT IT LOOKS LIKE:
Creamy-white flowers, June to August.

⁕❧FIRST-AID BOX❧⁕

In 1839, a German chemist dug up references to meadowsweet's healing properties in a mediaeval herbarium, and discovered that it contained salicin, an anti-inflammatory. After tinkering with the properties of meadowsweet, they came up with salicylic acid, which is patented by Bayer as the drug we now know as aspirin.

The meadowsweet flower head contains salicylic acid, from which aspirin can be synthesised. A cordial from meadowsweet tastes rather like barley water, and is a refreshing drink, as well as a natural cure for stomach upsets such as diarrhoea, ulcers, heartburn and hyperacidity, as the combination of constituents in meadowsweet act to protect the inner lining of the stomach and intestines while still providing the anti-inflammatory benefits of aspirin.

first aid.

ELDERFLOWER
{Sambucus nigra}

Elderflower is the queen of wild blossoms, the one that gets everyone started on cordials. The elder is one of our most common trees/shrubs, and, in late, spring and early summer, elderflowers are everywhere, even in the middle of our cities. Once you start looking for elderflowers, you'll wonder how you ever missed them; in fact, there is probably an elder tree growing on a street corner, roadside or back alley within walking distance of where you are sitting. On a warm day in late spring/early summer, the sweet aroma of elderflower hits you as you walk by – so if you've been strolling along in an iPod-induced stupor, the elderflower scent will knock you back into the natural world.

IDENTIFICATION

FIND IT HERE: Elder grows on roadsides, in fields, hedgerows, gardens and parks.
WHAT IT LOOKS LIKE:
Elder is a ubiquitous, fast-growing tall tree/ shrub (which can grow up to 10 metres high) with large, dark-green, slightly toothed leaves. It starts to flower in May – although the flowers tend to be at their best in June and July – and is covered in a profusion of tiny creamy-white, flat-headed flowers (or umbels), in clusters the size of a fist, that are unmistakably fragrant. In autumn, it produces small dark purple berries (elderberries) that grow in clusters in the same way.
WHAT IT CAN BE CONFUSED WITH:
Elder grows so prolifically that, once you know what it looks like, you won't mistake it for anything else. However, make sure that you pick from established hedgerows, from the native purple-berried *Sambucus nigra*, and not from the red-berried invader from Central Asia, *Sambucus racemosa*, which has been planted by foresters on the edges of plantations and after clear-cutting, as it is very fast growing. Fruit from the red elderberry can cause stomach upsets and the seeds are thought to be poisonous.

The origin of the name 'elder' is Anglo-Saxon and stems from the word '*aeld*', meaning fire; the hollowed-out stems were used to start fires. Elder trees are found almost everywhere in Europe, West Asia and right across North America. Elder is steeped in myth and folklore: in the Isle of Man, every cottage had an elder growing outside its front door to ward off witches; in Russia, an elder tree in this position was thought to ward off unwanted or evil spirits.

BLOSSOM CORDIAL *Makes 1.5 litres/2–3 pints*

Elderflower cordial has now found its place on the shelf in supermarkets, alongside the most exclusive royal cordials and syrups in the land, all available for a large king's ransom.

Of course, making it yourself is far more enjoyable and the end result much better (and infinitely cheaper) than any shop version. One of the joys of making lots of cordials is that you can store them for a taste of early summer throughout the winter, with a smell so evocative that it will make you want to run upstairs and put your shorts on.

This basic cordial recipe can be used not just for elderflower, but for all the blossoms we have mentioned.

All it takes to make cordial is a bit of forward planning. Instead of taking all your bottles for recycling, start saving any useful screw-top or stopper-top glass or heavy-duty plastic bottles. Cordials and syrups are an excellent cupboard/freezer item that can be added to various dishes long after the flowers have dropped, turned into berries and fallen to the ground. For example, sponge cakes and puddings can be given a lift by adding a couple of handfuls of flower heads, when in season, or a dash of syrup in mid-winter.

Dare to use it however you choose – if you're making anything sweet that calls for sugar, you can try elderflower syrup instead. Unseasonal, yes, but its carbon footprint is as dainty as a sugar-plum fairy.

25–50 CLUSTERS BLOSSOM (BLACKTHORN, ELDERFLOWER,
CRAB APPLE, MEADOWSWEET ETC.)

3 UNWAXED LEMONS

500g/1lb CASTER SUGAR

1.5 litres/2–3 pints BOILING WATER

60–80g/2–3oz CITRIC ACID, IF YOU ARE GOING TO STORE THE COR-
DIAL FOR A WHILE

You will also need the following tools: glass bottles with stoppers or screw tops (or plastic bottles, if you intend to freeze the cordial); grater; saucepan; large bowl; weighing scales; measuring jug; food processor; funnel; cotton muslin (or fine sieve or clean cotton handkerchief).

1. Shake the blossom sprays free of any small bugs. The number of blossom heads you use will vary according to the blossom. With large blossom heads, such as elderflower, use around 25, whereas with smaller blossom heads, such as meadowsweet, use more, roughly a loosely packed carrier bag-full.

2. Grate the peel of the lemons, then cut two of them into slices, and put to one side.

3. Make a syrup by putting the sugar into a pan and pouring the boiling water over it, stirring until all the sugar has dissolved. Keep it hot.

4. Put the third lemon into the food processor with a little of the sugar syrup and whiz it for about one minute.

5. Trim the flower heads into a large bowl, and add the grated lemon peel, the lemon slices, puréed lemon and citric acid.

6. Pour the hot sugar syrup over the flower heads, stir well and leave to cool. The mixture should be left for 24–48 hours, stirring occasionally.

7. Strain the mixture through the muslin, handkerchief or fine sieve, squeezing any excess moisture out of the flowers.

8. Pour into bottles and store.

Note: The basic sugar-syrup mixture can be adapted to make exotic sorbets out of edible flowers (see below and Pages 62 and 65).

WILD NETTLE AND BLACKCURRANT LEAF CORDIAL *Makes 1.5 litres/2–3 pints*

This is not strictly a flower cordial, but it is made at the same time of year. This old English beverage is mellow and fruity, not unlike a sauvignon blanc wine, but without the alcohol. Make sure that the leaves are freshly picked to ensure maximum flavour. Wild nettle and blackcurrant leaf cordial is good for asthma, hayfever and eczema, as well as being good for the immune system.

1kg/2lb GRANULATED SUGAR
500ml/17fl oz BOILING WATER
40g/1½oz CITRIC ACID
100g/3½oz NETTLE TIPS
100g/3½oz YOUNG BLACKCURRANT LEAVES

1. In a large saucepan, combine the water, sugar and citric acid, mixing together until all the sugar has dissolved. Bring to boiling point, and boil rapidly for a few minutes.

2. Add all the leaves and remove immediately from heat.

3. Leave in a cool dark place for 5–7 days, stirring intermittently.

4. Strain through cotton muslin, a clean cotton handkerchief or fine sieve.

5. Bottle and keep in the fridge.

SILVY'S GORSE FLOWER SYRUP CORDIAL AND SORBET *Makes 6–8 servings.*

We make tea from gorse flowers but think this recipe is interesting. Silvy Weatherall, an artist and cook, and her daughter, Ida, made up gorse-flower sorbet, which has a lovely meady taste. You can use any blossom and get your friends guessing what the flavour is.

600ml/21fl oz WATER
250g/½lb CASTER SUGAR
Zest one ORANGE
Juice one LEMON

4 handfuls **GORSE FLOWER, OR** 2 handfuls **FLOWER BLOSSOM, SUCH AS ELDERFLOWER, BLACKTHORN, APPLE ETC.**

1. In a large saucepan, mix together the sugar and water until all the sugar has dissolved, then bring the syrup to boil, and boil rapidly for 7 minutes.

2. Add the rest of the ingredients and, off the heat, let steep for 5 minutes or so.

3. Strain through cotton muslin, a clean cotton handkerchief or fine sieve, and use as a syrup, or freeze as for sorbet.

COURGETTE AND PECORINO SALAD WITH ELDERFLOWER VINAIGRETTE

Elderflower cordial incorporated into vinaigrette is delicious on this summer salad. If you can't find any ripe pears, don't worry, it's delicious without them too.

ELDERFLOWER CORDIAL
WHITE-WINE VINEGAR
OLIVE OIL
SEA SALT AND FRESHLY GROUND BLACK PEPPER
MUSTARD

1. Combine one part elderflower cordial and one part white-wine vinegar to two parts thin olive oil.

2. Add salt and pepper and mustard to taste.

TRY THE VINAIGRETTE ON THIS COMBINATION OF FLAVOURS:
YOUNG YELLOW AND GREEN COURGETTES, SLICED THINLY
Zest 1 **RIPE PEAR, CUT UP**
PECORINO CHEESE, GRATED ROUGHLY
YOUNG SALAD LEAVES
UNWAXED LEMON

BLACKCURRANT LEAF SORBET *Makes 6–8 servings.*

2 large handfuls **YOUNG BLACKCURRANT LEAVES**
600ml/1 pint **COLD WATER**
225g/8oz **SUGAR**
Juice 3 **LEMONS**
1 **EGG WHITE (OPTIONAL)**

1. Crush the blackcurrant leaves tightly in your hand, and rub your hands together a couple of times to release the aroma.

2. Put the crushed leaves into a stainless-steel saucepan with the cold water and sugar.

3. Stir to dissolve the sugar, bring slowly to the boil, then simmer for 2–3 minutes.

4. Allow the mixture to cool completely, then add the lemon juice.

5. Strain through cotton muslin, a clean cotton handkerchief or fine sieve.

6. Pour the juice into a stainless-steel or plastic container and freeze for about 4–5 hours or until semi-frozen.

7. Remove from the freezer and whisk until smooth, then return to the freezer.

8. Whisk again when almost frozen and fold in one stiffly beaten egg white, if desired.

9. Alternatively, for steps 6–8 above: If you have a food processor, simply freeze the sorbet completely in a stainless-steel or plastic bowl, then break into large pieces and whiz up in the food processor for a few seconds. Add one slightly beaten egg white, if desired, and whiz again for another few seconds, then return to the bowl and freeze again until needed.

10. Keep in the freezer until needed.

11. Serve in chilled glasses or chilled white china bowls or on pretty plates lined with fresh blackcurrant leaves.

ELDERFLOWER AND POLENTA CAKE *Makes 10 servings.*

We discovered the elderflower and polenta combination on a visit to Glass & Thompson, a bijoux coffee shop in Edinburgh's New Town, sandwiched between art galleries. They had just introduced it on to the menu, and it was a much needed shot of sweetness, particularly on a blustery October day. So we recreated it.

300g/10½oz	UNSALTED BUTTER, SOFTENED (REMEMBER TO TAKE THE BUTTER OUT OF THE FRIDGE AHEAD OF TIME!)
300g/10½oz	CASTER SUGAR
75g/2½oz	PLAIN FLOUR
4	EGGS
225g/8oz	FINE GROUND POLENTA
Zest 2	LEMONS
2 tsp	BAKING POWDER
1 pinch	SEA SALT
2 tbsp	ELDERFLOWER SYRUP
2 heads	ELDERFLOWER BLOSSOM TO GARNISH (IF THEY ARE STILL IN SEASON)

1. Preheat the oven to 325°F/170°C/Gas 3.
2. Butter the inside of an 8-inch/20-centimetre cake tin or flan dish.
3. Beat together the butter and sugar in a bowl or in the food processor until pale and fluffy.
4. Gradually stir in the flour.
5. Beat in the eggs one at a time.
6. Stir in the polenta, lemon zest, baking powder, salt and elderflower syrup, then tip into the cake tin or flan dish.
7. Bake for 45 minutes, or until cooked (test with a skewer in the middle – if it comes out clean, it's cooked).
8. Turn out on to a wire rack to cool.
9. To serve, shake the elderflowers over the top.

ELDERFLOWER FLAT BREAD *Makes one large loaf.*

Italians are great foragers, and wild foods of all kinds are incorporated into many traditional Italian recipes. This is a traditional Tuscan bread using elderflowers. Rosemary leaves, or a wild herb such as thyme can be substituted, in the same quantity as the elderflowers.

160ml/5fl oz **LUKEWARM WATER**
30g/1oz **FRESH CAKE YEAST, OR** 2 packets **ACTIVE DRY YEAST**
300g/10oz **PLAIN FLOUR**
1 pinch **SEA SALT**
90g/3oz **ELDERFLOWERS, ALL STEMS REMOVED**
2 tbsp **EXTRA-VIRGIN OLIVE OIL**

1. Place lukewarm water into a bowl, sprinkle the yeast on top and let it stand until dissolved and foamy – this should take about 10 minutes.

2. Put all the flour in a pile on a clean work surface, and make a well in the centre. Pour the salt, elderflowers and yeast mixture into the well, and whisk in the flour with a fork until all the liquid is absorbed and the dough forms a soft ball. Alternatively, you can make the dough in a large mixing bowl.

3. Flour a clean work surface, and knead the dough until elastic: again about 10 minutes.

4. Shape the dough into a ball , then put it in a lightly floured bowl, covered with plastic wrap, leave at room temperature for about an hour. After this time it should have doubled in size.

5. Preheat the oven to 400°F/200°C/Gas 6.

6. Turn the dough on to a floured work surface again, and knead briefly, then pat down with the palms of your hands into a 9-inch/23-centimetre-round cake, then turn into a floured 9-inch/23-centimetre cake tin.

7. Make several shallow indentations in the dough with your fingertips, and sprinkle the dough with the olive oil.

8. Bake the bread until golden, about 30 minutes.

9. Let the bread cool on a wire rack.

ELDERFLOWER SORBET *Makes 6–8 servings.*

300ml/½ pint **WATER**
250g/½lb **SUGAR**
12 **ELDERFLOWER HEADS**
2 **LEMONS** (zest and juice)
1 glass **WHITE WINE**
2 **EGG WHITES**

1. Boil the sugar and water together for 5 minutes in a saucepan.

2. Take off the heat and infuse the elderflowers in the still-hot liquid for about 30 minutes.

3. When cool, strain off the elderflowers.

4. Add the lemon zest and juice and white wine to the elderflower infusion.

5. Pour into a tub and freeze completely.

6. When frozen, break up roughly and put into a food processor with the egg whites, or, if processing by hand, beat the egg whites until stiff and then fold into the elderflower ice.

7. Process until it's light and creamy.

8. Refreeze, and remove from freezer 10 minutes before serving.

If you are making this out of season, and don't have any fresh elderflower heads, instead of making the elderflower infusion, you could try using elderflower cordial: put 4 tablespoons of cordial in with the water, lemon zest and juice and white wine, then freeze.

The addition of a little bit of tequila when served is recommended.

DRINKS

For armchair chefs who prefer to dream than cook, there is the drinks option: a drop of this and a twist of that, some fizz and a few plink-plonks and there you have it! A drop or two of elderflower cordial adds a little something that is new and fresh. For your ultimate quick fix, try a cordial with anything you happen to have in the cupboard, e.g. white wine, vodka, gin or champagne.

ELDERFLOWER CHAMPAGNE

A friend of mine was served elderflower champagne at a wedding in the Cotswolds and it was as popular as the expensive French variety!

36	ELDERFLOWER HEADS
2	LEMONS (SLICED)
3.6 litres/6 pints	WATER
700g/1lb 10oz	SUGAR
2 tbsp	WHITE-WINE VINEGAR

1. Put the elderflower heads and lemons into a bucket, pour the water on top of them and leave to soak for 24–36 hours.

2. Strain through a muslin (or fine sieve) and add the sugar and white-wine vinegar.

3. Stir until the sugar is completely dissolved, and pour into screw-top bottles (empty screw-top wine bottles are fine provided you rinse them with boiling water to sterilise them).

4. Leave tops slightly loose for 10–14 days.

5. Keep for 2–3 months before drinking.

ELDERFLOWER MARTINI

30ml/1oz	ELDERFLOWER CORDIAL
30ml/1oz	(BOMBAY SAPPHIRE) GIN
30ml/1oz	CINZANO, DRY VERMOUTH
	LIME (zest and juice)

1. Combine all the ingredients, except the lime zest, in a cocktail shaker half filled with ice cubes.

2. Shake to chill, and mix and serve immediately in a cocktail glass with a twist of lime zest.

EATING FLOWERS

My stepmother associates elderflower fritters with reaching a higher spiritual plane: she came back from a yoga trip to a Tuscan monastery having had a mind-and-body workout. Salads dripping with extra-virgin olive oil, basil, ripe tomatoes and elderflower fritters had changed her life, and she was ready for the post-holiday blues.

Anxious not to let this happen (as I didn't want to deal with the fall-out), we tentatively tried to recreate this dish and are happy to report that elderflowers fare just as well – and are just as exotic – in the watery British sun as they do under a Tuscan sky.

Our first foraging adventure involved eating flowers – elderflower fritters, which came close to a perfect moment. We took our kids into our local communal gardens after school one day, picked a whole load of elderflowers, then came home and cooked up elderflower fritters. The kids loved them straight from the pan, piping hot and dipped in icing sugar. The first taste is a food sensation that you'll never forget. The novelty of eating flowers is not to be underestimated. We have since tried it with all sorts of other flowers, such as dandelions, lime flowers, clover flowers, and have got into the habitat of using flowers – or their essence – in lots of our cooking. Lavender ice cream, dandelion and clover syrups, wild garlic flowers in salads, borage flowers in cocktails. The list is endless.

FLOWER FRITTERS *Makes 16 fritters.*

FOR THE BATTER:

1 **EGG**
225ml/8fl oz **ICED WATER**
140g/ 5oz **PLAIN FLOUR**
1 pinch **SEA SALT**

FOR THE FRITTERS:
VEGETABLE OIL
16 heads **ELDERFLOWERS**
ICING SUGAR
FRESH LEMON

1. Make the batter by, first, beating the egg, then slowly adding the water, continuing to beat the mixture as you do so.

2. Slowly sift flour and salt into the egg-and-water mixture, whisking to make sure there are no lumps.

3. Fill a wide, deepish pan or wok with vegetable oil to come two to three centimetres up the sides, and heat almost to smoking point.

4. Dip the elderflower heads in the batter and fry a few at a time until golden-brown.

5. Drain on a kitchen towel while you fry the rest.

6. Sprinkle the fritters with sugar and serve with a twist of lemon while still hot.

❀ EDIBLE FLOWERS ❀

Flower	Use in...	Tastes like...
Rocket	Salads	Nutty, spicy flavour
Borage	Salads, in cool drinks	Cucumber taste; remove thorny backs
Wild garlic	Salads	Garlicky
Onion grass	Salads, stir-fries	
Calendula	Salads, teas	Spicy, tangy
Lavender	Salads, teas, sorbets, ice creams	Use lightly as has strong perfumed taste.
Marigold	Salads, teas	Spicy to bitter
Nasturtium	Salads	Mildly pungent to peppery
Pansy	Salads	Mildly sweet to tart flavour
Rose	Salads, teas, infusions	Sweet aromatic flavour; just use petals
Courgette	Batter	Crisp and fresh tasting
Thyme	Salads, teas	Lemony; adds a light scent
Dandelion	Salads, batter, teas	Honey-like scent and taste
Clover, red and white	Salads, teas	Taste of sweet nectar
Lime blossom (Linden blossom)	Teas	Light and refreshing
Fruit blossoms – elderflower, crab, apple (not bird cherry)	Batter, cordials, sorbets, syrups	Aromatic and delicate fragrance

Eat flowers only when you are positive they are edible. Some flowers are poisonous!

- If you have hay fever, asthma or allergies do not eat flowers.
- Do not eat flowers from side of the road, they may be contaminated.
- Remove the pistils and stamens from flowers before eating, eating only the petals.
- There are many different varieties of flowers; they taste different according to where they have grown.
- Introduce flowers into your diet in small quantities.

WILD FLOWER, LEAF AND BERRY TEAS

Infusions or tisanes can be made from fresh or dried leaves of wild plants, flowers, herbs and berries. They can have remarkable tonic-giving and health-giving effects.

> LEAVES: ANGELICA, BILBERRY, BLACKCURRANT, DANDE-
> LION, ELDER, HOP, LEMON BALM, PINE NEEDLES, WILD
> STRAWBERRY.
> FLOWERS/BERRIES: BORAGE, CAMOMILE, ELDERFLOW-
> ERS, FEVERFEW, HAWTHORN, JUNIPER BERRIES, LADY'S
> MANTLE, LAVENDER, LIME, MARIGOLD, MARJORAM,
> MEADOWSWEET, MINT, NETTLE, ROSE, ROSE HIPS,
> SWEET CICELY, THYME, YARROW.

1. Strip the flowers/leaves off their stalks and dry in the sun's rays, or on newspaper in a warm, dry place, for 2–3 days, turning them at intervals until brittle.

2. When dry, store in paper bags, tied tightly shut, or in airtight jars.

3. When making tea, use 1½ teaspoons chopped dried flowers/leaves per cup. If using fresh ingredients: first, bruise the flowers/leaves, then pour boiling water over them, and leave the infusion to steep for 7–10 minutes.

4. Strain, and sweeten with honey if desired.

LIME OR LINDEN
{*Tilia europa*}

There are several species of lime or linden tree. I first tasted lime-blossom tea when a French cousin of mine took some dried lime blossom out of a large sack hanging on his kitchen wall and made it into the most refreshing aromatic tea I had ever tasted. Not realising, I'd been walking straight past the lime blossom every day while walking the dog in the park.

Highly esteemed in France for its digestive properties, it is known there as *tilleul*. Dry the flowers for tea, or use fresh to flavour desserts. The young leaves can be eaten in sandwiches!

IDENTIFICATION

FIND IT HERE:
Often found in park avenues, gardens and mixed woodland.
WHAT IT LOOKS LIKE:
The leaves, which unfold in early spring, are soft and waxy, broad bright lime green, and are often covered in resin. The flowers are sweet scented and yellow, hanging down from the tree in clusters, and can be gathered in June and July.

DANDELION
{Taraxacum officinale}

Nasturtiums and roses may be more flashy, but it is the humble dandelion flower that will give you the most health benefits. ***Taraxacum officinale*** (dandelion) derives from the Greek words '***taraxos***', meaning 'disorder', and '***akos***', meaning 'remedy'. The title '***officinale***' indicates that the dandelion was officially listed as a medicinal.

DANDELION BLOSSOM SYRUP (OR CLOVER BLOSSOM SYRUP)

Dandelion syrup has a taste of nut and vanilla. It may sound rather time consuming, but use child labour – it's amazing how quickly four children can fill 4 cups full of clover heads, especially when a little bit of competition is introduced. For a healthy tonic, add one tablespoon of syrup to a glass of water and drink daily during the winter.

4 cups	**DANDELION FLOWERS**
1/1¾pints	**WATER**
900g/2lb	**SUGAR**
½	**LEMON OR ORANGE, CHOPPED, PEEL ETC.**

1. Put the dandelion flowers in a large saucepan and add the water.

2. Bring just to the boil, turn off heat, cover and leave to sit overnight.

3. Strain and press liquid out of spent flowers. Discard the flowers and retain the liquid.

4. To the dandelion-flower-infused liquid, add sugar and sliced fruit and heat slowly, stirring now and again, until reduced to a thick honey-like syrup.

5. Make sure you wipe the cooker immediately as sugar syrup will harden.

6. Store in a tightly sealed jar in the refrigerator.

By freezing some of the dandelion-flower-infused liquid, you can make syrup later on in the year when the dandelions are not flowering. Clover-blossom syrup can be made by using clover flowers instead of dandelion flowers.

DANDELION BAKLAVA

We suggest you buy ready-made filo sheets that take the faff out of this recipe.

2 cups **WALNUTS OR PECANS**
1 tsp **SUGAR**
½ tsp **CINNAMON**
½ tsp **NUTMEG**
25g/1oz **BUTTER**
½ box **FILO LEAVES**
190ml/6½fl oz **DANDELION-BLOSSOM SYRUP** (SEE PAGE 71)

1. Combine the nuts with the sugar and spices.

2. Melt the butter.

3. Layer 8 sheets of filo into a greased 23-centimetre by 33-centimetre (9-inch by 13-inch) pan, brushing every other sheet with the butter using a pastry brush.

4. Sprinkle evenly with half of the nut mixture.

5. Layer the rest of the filo sheets, then brush the top layer generously with butter.

6. Cut the baklava into squares with a sharp knife before baking, then bake in the oven at 375°F/190°C/Gas 5 for half an hour, until slightly browned.

7. Remove from the oven, and pour the dandy blossom syrup over the hot baklava, making sure the syrup is at room temperature.

DANDELION LEAF TEA

This tea is an extremely effective diuretic. It is wise to up your quota of potassium-rich foods, such as bananas, apples, oranges, carrots and potatoes, when using a diuretic to preserve essential salts.

1. Pour boiling water over 2 teaspoons of dried (or 4 teaspoons of freshly chopped) dandelion leaves, and steep for 10 minutes.

LAVENDER
{Lavandula angustifolia}

Lavender is more usually associated with perfumed soap and potpourri than eating. But lavender makes a wonderful infusion, and great ice creams and sorbets.

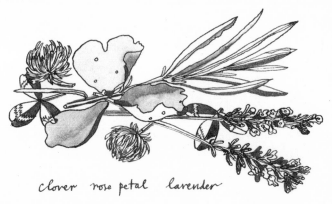

clover   rose petal   lavender

LYN'S LAVENDER ICE CREAM *Makes 6 servings.*

I have struggled with the smell of lavender since it was dabbed on my temples during labour – it has too many painful memories. Until recently that is. I have found that I can't inhale it, but I can eat it. Lyn, our communal gardener, promised me a recipe that would not trigger contractions. She carried the recipe in the back of her wheelbarrow until she saw me next, and told me it would not disappoint. How right she was: now a family favourite.

1 small bunch	LAVENDER
225g/8oz	CASTER SUGAR
100 ml/3½fl oz	WATER
450ml/16fl oz	SINGLE CREAM
1	VANILLA POD
6	EGG YOLKS
300ml/10fl oz	DOUBLE CREAM

1. Pull a generous handful of lavender off its stalk with the aid of a fork or knife, and place in bowl.

2. In a saucepan, dissolve the caster sugar in the water and bring to the boil, then pour over the flowers. Leave to infuse for one hour, then strain.

3. Heat the single cream and vanilla pod gently to a point when a skin forms.

4. Beat the egg yolks and add the heated cream slowly with a whisk, then return to saucepan and stir until it makes a custard. Leave it off the heat to cool.

5. Whip up the double cream and fold the custard into it, adding the lavender water.

6. Put the mixture into a plastic dish and freeze for one and a half hours.

7. Beat up the mixture with a spoon and refreeze, leaving for another one and a half hours.

8. Beat again and refreeze and leave one last time for one and a half hours.

ROSE
{Rosa cana}

Rose petals from the hedgerow are fun and easy to collect, but there is no reason why petals should not be gathered from other sources, as long as they are picked away from obvious pollution. In order to attempt to bottle or preserve the smell of summer, the more heavily scented the rose, the stronger the taste will be.

We have incorporated a few recipes that are both unusual and aromatic. Try adding petals to pancake mixtures, frozen yoghurts, salads, milk shakes – you will be amazed at the calming effect it has.

The following rose recipes are adapted from Rosamund Richardson's book, **Hedgerow Cookery**. Tried and tested, they are exquisite and simple to follow.

ROSE PETAL JELLY

500g/1lb **COOKING APPLES**
1 handful **ROSE PETALS**
WATER
SUGAR

1. Peel and chop the cooking apples, and stew them gently in enough water to cover.

2. Strain through a jelly bag overnight, setting the liquid aside in a measuring jug.

3. For every 600 millilitres (1 pint) of liquid, add 325 grams (11½ ounces) of sugar, then dissolve over a low heat and bring to the boil.

4. Take the base of the petals off – they can be a bit tougher – and add the petals to the apple syrup.

5. Boil until the jelly reaches setting point. To test for this, remove the pan from the heat, then place a few drops of the jelly on to a cold plate, and allow to cool. If the jelly has formed a skin that wrinkles when a finger is pushed gently into it, then the jelly will set. If this doesn't happen, boil the jelly for a little longer and retest.

6. Strain through a jelly bag or muslin and put into sterilised jars.

ROSE PETAL SYRUP

Delicious with ice cream or to flavour a cake in the middle of winter.

225g/8oz **SUGAR**
500ml/17½fl oz **WATER**
½ **LEMON, SQUEEZED**
½ **ORANGE, SQUEEZED**
2 cups **ROSE PETALS**

1. Put the sugar, water and fruit juices into a pan over a low heat, then add the rose petals.

2. Keeping the pan on a low heat, stir constantly for about half an hour, making sure it does not reach boiling point.

3. Set the liquid aside, and, when cool, pour into sterilised bottles or jars.

ROSE ICE CREAM

½ cup **DARK-RED ROSE PETALS**
150ml/¼ pint **ROSE PETAL SYRUP**
150ml/¼ pint **DOUBLE CREAM**
40g/1½oz **ICING SUGAR, SIFTED**
2 **EGG WHITES**
12 **CRYSTALLISED ROSE PETALS (SEE PAGE 77)**

1. Wash the petals and shake them dry.

2. Liquidise them for a minute with the rose petal syrup.

3. Beat together the cream and the icing sugar, until thick.

4. Stir the rose mixture into the cream mixture.

5. Beat the egg whites until stiff, then fold into the cream mixture and put into an ice-cream container, cover and freeze.

6. When serving, decorate with the crystallised rose petals.

ROSE WATER

Rose petals
Water

1. Check over your rose petals and cover with boiling water. The strength of the rose water will be determined by the ratio of petals to water, and you may need to add more petals if they are delicately scented.
2. Cover and leave overnight.
3. Strain the water through a muslin or sieve, making sure that all the moisture is squeezed out of the petals.
4. Pour into sterilised bottles.

CRYSTALLISED ROSE PETALS

This method can be used with any flowers or leaves you wish, e.g. primroses, garden violets. Great for making iced cakes look decorative through the flowerless months.

Egg white
Edible flower petals (or leaves) of choice
Caster sugar

1. Beat the egg white until it forms stiff peaks.
2. Dip the clean and dry petals or leaves into the egg white (holding with tweezers for best effect), making sure that the entire surface is covered.
3. Sprinkle both sides with the caster sugar and dry on a rack in a slow oven (250°F/ 130°C/Gas ½) for 2–3 hours.
4. Store in sealed jars or containers.

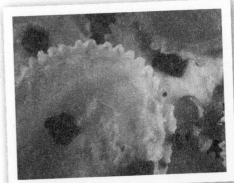

5 STALKING THE SEA GREENS

{ Alexanders, Scots Lovage, Pignut, Orache, Fat Hen, Sea Beet, Rock Samphire, Marsh Samphire }

ALEXANDERS THE GREAT

Date: *May Bank Holiday*
Place: *East coast*
Weather: *Glorious*
Objective: *Sea greens*

Today is my birthday, and my daughter, Lydia, insists that we have to bake a birthday cake. No cake, no birthday, is the eight-year-old logic, even if it means baking your own birthday cake. Our friend Nick, a chef, is coming over for tea with his wife and their two kids, and, as I contemplate whether I can serve up a Victoria sponge prepared in the food processor to a chef, I decide to send Xa a text: 'Sea Greens await. Enjoy Skye'.

Xa sends a text message back: 'Have eaten pignut, and interviewed the hippie. Weather superb.'

Xa's text message perhaps needs some explanation. We are not yet desperate enough to spend the weekend sampling the testicles of swine. We're into good food, not survival. But it was her first pignut. The aforementioned 'pignut' is the tuber of **Conopodium majus**, a plant that looks like cow parsley, except that the leaves are more feathery. It grows in meadows and pastureland, and the tubers taste a bit like hazelnuts. You have to get the landowner's permission first before you dig them up.

Lydia and I throw the sponge mixture in the food processor and stomp off towards a rocky headland in search of something worth foraging. Along the path beside the coastal dunes of the fourth hole of the golf course, I see a bushy plant with large, yellow-green clusters of flowers, growing to shoulder height, nestling in the long grass. I pick, carefully, to make sure I have flower, stalk and leaves, to take home to identify. The leaves are dark green and glossy, and grow in groups of three.

However, after closer inspection, I am pretty sure it is Alexanders, described in some books as 'rare in Scotland' – and only found on the coast.

It is time to send another text to Xa on Skye (not that I'm competitive or anything): 'I have found Alexanders! Will bring back to Edinburgh for second opinion!'

Back home on Monday evening, I arrive at Xa's door like the Green Goddess, with a bag full of green gifts, unable to wait any longer.

Down in the kitchen, a second opinion quickly confirms the diagnosis as **Smyrnium olusatrum** – Alexanders.

ALEXANDERS

{Smyrnium olusatrum}

Like many 'wild' plants in Britain, Alexanders is an ex-garden pot-herb, which had been commonly planted in kitchen gardens throughout the 17th century, but had fallen out of fashion by the 18th century, and is now growing wild. The Romans first brought Alexanders to this country – its common name comes from Alexander the Great. Its latin name '**Smryrnium**' comes from it's myrrh-like smell.

IDENTIFICATION

FIND IT HERE:

Alexanders grows by the sea, in hedgerows, woodlands and roadsides, on sandy soil. Alexanders is one of the few greens that grows all winter long. The leaves can be picked and eaten throughout the winter. The plant flowers between May and June, so the stalks and leaves are best eaten before then.

WHAT IT LOOKS LIKE:

Like all umbellifers, it is best identified when it has flowered, so that there is no mistake. (This is a shame, because it tastes better before it has flowered!) The key identifiers for Alexanders are the leaves, which are shiny dark green three-lobed leaves, and the flat-headed flowers, which are a startling yellowy-green.

COMMONSENSE TIPS

• Select the youngest, pinkest-looking stems, as they get a bit woody once the plant is older and in flower.

• When you know what it looks like, and where it grows, then it can be picked in spring, before the flowers come out.

COOKING WITH ALEXANDERS

Alexanders is a very versatile herb – its stems, leaves, flower buds, flower heads and roots can all be used – and it has one of the most unusual tastes that we have experienced. While it looks rather like small celery or hollow asparagus, it doesn't taste like either of those.

Pick out the youngest-looking, pinkish stems. Then cut them into asparagus-sized strips, and steam gently over boiling water for a few minutes. The water turns an alarming blue colour, as the pigment comes out, and the strips of Alexanders turn from pinkish to bright green. Drained and slathered with butter, Alexanders is as tasty as the first pickings of asparagus.

The young leaves and flower buds can also be eaten. The leaves add a delicate flavour to béchamel sauces, and the buds can be added to salads. The flower heads themselves can be used for savoury fritters (see recipe for Spring Green Tempura, Page 37). The roots can be cooked in the same way as parsnips, or used instead of the potatoes to bulk up a soup (see Nettle Soup, Page 23).

We picked fresh young Alexanders leaves in mid-December, when everything else seemed dead, and combined the leaves with onion and garlic and a large cooking apple, some chicken stock and cream, to make a very distinctive tasting soup with a lemony tang.

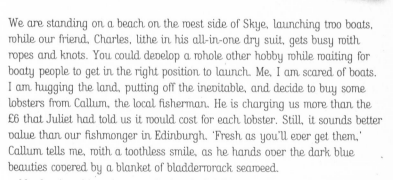

LOVE THAT LOVAGE

Date: *May Bank Holiday*
Place: *Isle of Skye*
Weather: *Glorious*
Objective: *Holidaying and stalking sea greens*

We are standing on a beach on the west side of Skye, launching two boats, while our friend, Charles, lithe in his all-in-one dry suit, gets busy with ropes and knots. You could develop a whole other hobby while waiting for boaty people to get in the right position to launch. Me, I am scared of boats. I am hugging the land, putting off the inevitable, and decide to buy some lobsters from Callum, the local fisherman. He is charging us more than the £6 that Juliet had told us it would cost for each lobster. Still, it sounds better value than our fishmonger in Edinburgh. 'Fresh as you'll ever get them,' Callum tells me, with a toothless smile, as he hands over the dark blue beauties covered by a blanket of bladderwrack seaweed.

My dog is poking about on the beach; I follow suit. I am feeling peckish and the men are still messing with yards of rope. I have read somewhere that sea legumes can push through at least 3 foot of shingle, so I start checking out the edible vegetation, as lunch is one hour away.

The first plant I see is bluish-grey leafed, with thick pinkish stalks. I strip off a leaf and inspect it; it smells salty - nothing too off-putting at this stage. I take a bite and wait for the taste of the sea to flood my senses. Incredibly, this plant tastes of my favourite crustacea, the oyster plant. The oyster plant (**Mertensia maritimum**) is rare in the British Isles, found only on a few stretches of coastal shingle in Scotland. I feel like a bird-spotter who's just

clocked a rare summer visitor. The oyster plant is extremely tasty, and I offer
my son a bite, who agrees that it is the next best thing to a real oyster.

Afloat at last, we make for the nearest island. Once on dry land, we set
about looking for wood on the white sandy beach. At the top of the island,
I find Scots lovage clinging perilously to a rock on the cliff-tops. Ever since
my stepmother put the cultivated version into her summer salads, I have
been fascinated by its unusual taste. Traditionally, it is a Highland cure-all.
I chew a leaf – it is extremely aromatic and a tiny bit bitter. I know that it is
good in stews or soups, so put some in my pocket to take home.

SCOTS LOVAGE

{Ligusticum scoticum}

Scots lovage, also known locally as scotch parsley or sea parsley, is the
wild cousin of cultivated lovage, but it has a wider, darker green leaf.

According to some writers, **Ligusticum scoticum** is named lovage because it is an aphrodisiac (as in loveage). But before you all rush out to the
nearest Scottish seashore, be warned that Scots lovage, like the cultivated
variety, has a strong, quite bitter flavour, that we happen to love, but may
not be to everybody's taste.

IDENTIFICATION

FIND IT HERE:
Scots lovage grows on seashores, usually
on shingle or rocky soil, or on sea cliffs.
As the name suggests, it grows in Scotland
(and Scandinavia) but not England.
WHAT IT LOOKS LIKE:
This perennial has green leaves similar in
fashion to flat-leaf parsley, but larger and
with toothed edges. It grows up to 60 centimetres tall, from April to October, produc-
ing yellow flowers in dense compound umbels, between July and August.
The stem is reddish-brown veined.
WHAT CAN IT BE CONFUSED WITH?:
Like all umbellifers, it is best to identify them when they are in flower.
Cultivated lovage (**Levisticum officinale**) is a pot-herb that was brought
to the British Isles from Southern Europe, and was a staple of 16th- and
17th-century kitchen gardens. However, it has since gone out of fashion,
especially among gardeners, as lovage, once established, is hard to control.

COOKING WITH LOVAGE

Lovage should be treated a bit like parsley, if adding to cooked dishes
– chopped, and added at the end of cooking.

WHITE BEAN AND CHICKEN STEW WITH LOVAGE AND DULSE *Makes 6 servings.*

12	CHICKEN THIGHS
2 tbsp	FLOUR
	SEA SALT AND FRESHLY GROUND BLACK PEPPER
	EXTRA-VIRGIN OLIVE OIL
1	ONION, SLICED
2 cloves	GARLIC, CRUSHED
2 cans	CANNELLNI OR BORLOTTI BEANS
1 can	TOMATOES
110–225ml/¼–½ pint	CHICKEN STOCK
2 small handfuls	DULSE, DRIED OR FRESH, FINELY CHOPPED
	LOVAGE, CHOPPED

1. Roll the chicken thighs in the flour, seasoned with salt
   and pepper.

2. Heat some olive oil in a heavy saucepan, then fry the
   chicken thighs in the pan for a few minutes, until brown,
   keeping them moving around so that they don't burn.
   Remove the chicken and put to one side.

3. Add more oil to the pan and fry the onion and garlic
   gently, until translucent, then remove from the heat.

4. Place the chicken thighs, onions and garlic in a cas-
   serole dish, then add the cannellini or borlotti beans,
   tomatoes, and enough chicken stock to cover the meat.

5. Add the dried or fresh dulse, place in an oven at
   300°F/150°C/Gas 2 and bake for one hour.

6. When cooked, remove from the oven, add chopped
   lovage and season to taste.

7. Serve with baked potatoes, or warm crusty bread, and a
   green salad.

PIGNUT

{Conopodium majus}

'I have not had a good square meal for a fortnight, I am living on pig-nuts. I shall have to turn vegetarian and eat my own tail!' said Tommy Brock.
It was not much of a joke, but it tickled old Mr Bouncer; because Tommy Brock was so fat and stumpy and grinning.
– *The Tale of Mr Tod*, Beatrix Potter

IDENTIFICATION

tools

FIND IT HERE:
Farmland, long grass, amongst buttercups, verges.

WHAT IT LOOKS LIKE:
A relative of the carrot family, this plant looks not unlike a smaller version of cow parsley. Umbels of tiny white flowers grow at the end of ridged stems. The leaves are feathery and usually quite thinly growing down the stem. The edible part, best dug out by using a pen-knife, is a little bigger than a hazelnut. It is dark brown and white, and you find it about 3 or 4 inches under the earth. It is not as oily as a tree nut, but nevertheless satisfying to eat once you have washed it.

WHAT IT CAN BE CONFUSED WITH:
Make sure that you have positively identified it for fear of confusing it with hemlock, wich is deadly.

COMMONSENSE TIPS

• It is now illegal to pick this plant on private farmland. Seek the farmer's permission first.

COMMON ORACHE *{Atriplex patula}*
FAT HEN *{Chenopodium album}*

Orache, along with Good King Henry (**Chenopodium bonus-henricus**) and Fat Hen (**Chenopodium album**) are all 'goose-foots' and are easy to spot due to the three-lobed shape of their leaves. Orache is commonly found beside the sea (or by the road due to winter salting) and Good King Henry and Fat Hen are common on waste ground in farmyards.

These greens, which have been around since the Stone Age, contain more iron and calcium than spinach, and are packed with vitamins B1 and B2.

IDENTIFICATION

FIND IT HERE:
Found on poor ground, roadside verges and seashore during April to October.
WHAT IT LOOKS LIKE:
Greenish white stems with pointed leaves and clusters of flowers on long spikes.
WHAT CAN IT BE CONFUSED WITH?:
There is one orache that doesn't taste good, *Atriplex littoralis*, but you'll know, because it smells foul. Trust your instinct on this one.

COMMONSENSE TIPS

• You can use this sea vegetable in purées, flavoured with nutmeg, or just in a stir-fry or savoury rice. Use as a stand-in for anything that includes spinach.

• Wash well to get rid of the salt.

FLINTSTONE'S SOUP *Makes 6 servings.*

We are calling this Flintstone's Soup because the sort of greens (orache, fat hen or sea beet) that are wilted into the soup have been around since Primitive man. It is the kind of soup that would get you through the night when the fire at the mouth of the cave has gone out.

1 large ONION, FINELY CHOPPED
2 cloves GARLIC, FINELY CHOPPED
EXTRA-VIRGIN OLIVE OIL
Handful BACON, LARDONS OR PANCETTA
Handful PARSLEY, FINELY CHOPPED
250g/½lb PUY OR BROWN LENTILS, WASHED AND CHECKED FOR GRIT
1 litre CHICKEN STOCK
2 or 3 handfuls ORACHE, FAT HEN OR SEA BEET, OR A COMBINATION, WASHED THOROUGHLY
LEMON, TO TASTE
MINT LEAVES

1. Fry the onion and garlic in the olive oil, until golden.

2. Add the bacon, lardons or pancetta and fry until brown, then add the parsley.

3. Throw in the lentils.

4. Add the stock and bring to boil. Simmer for approximately 30 minutes.

5. Meanwhile, put the washed greens in a steamer and cook for 2 minutes, then squeeze excess moisture out and add to the lentil pot.

6. Before serving, add a squeeze of lemon to taste and torn-up mint leaves.

7. Eat with crusty bread.

STONE AGE BEACH DIET

- The Stone Age diet was a varied and wholesome one that would put many of us to shame today. Archaeological research has suggested that the diet was varied and fairly rich in minerals and nutrients.

- Our early ancestors lived mostly by the coast, eating fish, seals, sea birds and eggs, seaweed, shellfish and the odd whale that happened by.

- They moved inland according to the season and availability of food source.

- Their diet included greens such as wild cabbage, white deadnettle, cleavers and several of the oraches, and salad leaves such as sorrel, wild garlic, tansy and mint, and fruits such as blueberries, as well as roots and seeds.

WILD GREENS SOUFFLÉ *Makes 4 servings.*

	BUTTER
85g/3oz	PARMESAN CHEESE, FRESHLY GRATED
2	SHALLOTS
175g/7oz	MIXTURE ORACHE, NETTLE TIPS AND GROUND ELDER, COOKED
	SEA SALT AND FRESHLY GROUND BLACK PEPPER
40g/2oz	FLOUR
300ml/½ pint	HOT MILK
4	EGGS, SEPARATED

1. Butter a soufflé dish and sprinkle with half of the Parmesan, and reserve the other half.

2. Sauté the chopped shallots in some butter, until soft, stir in the mixed leaves, and cook gently over a low heat, then season to taste.

3. In another pan, melt some more butter, add the flour and stir in the hot milk, until the mixture thickens.

4. Take the pan off the heat, and beat the egg yolks into the sauce slowly, then add the shallot-and-leaf mixture.

5. Beat the egg whites with a pinch of salt, until stiff, then fold into the shallot-and-leaf mixture, half at a time, and pour into the prepared soufflé dish.

6. Sprinkle with the rest of the Parmesan and cook in a hot oven, 375°F/190°C/Gas 5, for 25–30 minutes.

SEASIDE SAVOURY RICE *Makes 4 servings.*

We found the orache without any difficulty, growing through the shingle and in the dunes. If orache is not available, you can improvise with any other spring greens, such as Fat Hen, Good King Henry or spinach, if you can't find any wild greens.

1 large handful	ORACHE LEAVES (OR OTHER SPRING GREENS), SHREDDED
1	ONION
2	CARROTS
2 tbsp	EXTRA-VIRGIN OLIVE OIL
29g/15oz	DULSE (SOAKED IN WATER FOR 10 MINUTES), SHREDDED
225g/8oz	BROWN RICE
500g/1lb	PRAWNS
1 tbsp	SOY SAUCE
2 leaves	SORREL, FINELY CHOPPED
1 small bunch	PARSLEY, CHOPPED
	SEA SALT AND FRESHLY GROUND BLACK PEPPER
1 knob	BUTTER

1. Wash the orache and remove leaves from stalks, chop the onion finely and cut the carrots into strips 4 centimetres (1½ inches) long.

2. Heat the olive oil in a pan, and add the onion, then sauté for a few minutes.

3. Add the carrots and dulse, and allow to simmer with the lid on for 10–15 minutes.

4. Meanwhile, put the rice in a pan and add enough cold water to cover, boil and simmer for approximately 10–15 minutes, until the rice is cooked.

5. Add the prawns, soy sauce, finely chopped sorrel and shredded orache to the carrot, onion and dulse mixture. Season with salt and pepper.

6. Drain the rice and mix in the butter.

7. To serve, spoon the rice on to a warmed plate and cover with the prawn and vegetable mixture, then stir in some parsley.

YOU CAN'T BEAT SEA BEET
SEA BEET
{*Beta vulgaris*}

We think that this green is the king of sea vegetables. After cooking, it still maintains its texture, rich and creamy, and is exquisite with fish or seafood. Rich in vitamins A and C.

IDENTIFICATION

FIND IT HERE:
A member of the **Chenopodiaceae** family, it is found on the shoreline, in old sea walls and on salt marshes from June to September.

WHAT IT LOOKS LIKE:
Its leaves are spear shaped and glossy and it grows up to three feet high. Leaves usually grow in a thick profusion.

COMMONSENSE TIPS

• Pick judiciously, and wait until leaves are a fair size, though not so big that they are too tough. Cut stalks with a knife, don't tear, and cook as spinach.

IN SEARCH OF ROCK-EDIBLES

Date: *7 July*
Place: *The most southerly tip of Galloway*
Weather: *Blue sky*
Objective: *Rock samphire*

From my cliff-top vantage point, there is nothing but the land mass of America out West. Robin Nicholson, a local farmer, has just pointed out the rocky crags where rock samphire grows, 50 feet below me. I have to believe that tartare sauce made with rock samphire is a taste sensation to die for – why else would I be launching myself off the sharp side of a cliff face to pick it?

Nicholson has told me that, as a young man, he used to clamber down the cliff with a gun tucked under his arm, he's also caught a record-breaking shark in the waters below, with nothing but a bamboo pole. I am carrying nothing but a plastic bag, and comfort myself with the thought that I couldn't fit a shark in it anyway.

I can only assume he is seeing what we're made of.

'Righto, I'm off. You're not scared are you?' he asks, as he rushes off to open up his plant nursery at 2 p.m.

'No! Of course not!' I reply indignantly.

Here goes. What will be, will be. I drop down over the heathery bank that falls sharply down to the large blackened boulders below. The sea is not yet at high tide, so at least I don't have to worry about surviving in the bitterly cold ocean; I'll come to a quick end being dashed upon the boulders instead.

I spy the bright green succulent shoots of rock samphire, with their lime-green flower heads. Rock samphire is not to be confused with marsh samphire or (or glasswort), which thrives in muddy estuaries or salt washes.

With small bunches of the samphire salted away in my bag, I scrabble back down to the bottom and make my ascent up the banks to safety and a drink of water.

I meet Fiona at the end of the cliff path – she has come to rescue me, concerned that I have taken so long. The kids, meanwhile, are happy as clams, dangling nets in rock pools.

Later that afternoon, we take a walk along the shingly beach to St Ninian's Cave. There, growing on the beach outside the Christian monk's refuge, is a large patch of rock samphire, beautifully accessible. But who cares, I'm alive!

Samphire

ROCK SAMPHIRE
{*Crithmum maritimum*}

IDENTIFICATION

FIND IT HERE:
Grows high up on rocks and cliffs, among the thrifts and pinks, and also on shingle.

WHAT IT LOOKS LIKE:
Bright green with rubbery, succulent shoots like spiky fingers, and flat yellow-green flower heads. Part of the *Umbelliferae* family, it grows up to 30 centimetres (12 inches) high, and flowers from June to August. It is aromatic and almost medicinal in its potency.

COMMONSENSE TIPS

• Pick the young shoots.

• Adult supervision! Stick to the beach preferably. This plant can be protected in some conservation areas.

ROCK SAMPHIRE TARTARE SAUCE *Makes 4–6 servings.*

HOME-MADE MAYONNAISE (SEE SEAFOOD MAYON-
NAISE PAGE 133)
ROCK SAMPHIRE PICKLE (SEE PAGE 93)

1. Make your Home-made Mayon-naise without adding too much vinegar.

2. Remove and drain a few pieces of Rock Samphire Pickle from your jar and chop into short pieces, then fold into the may-onnaise.

Samphire and Tartare

ROCK SAMPHIRE PICKLE *Makes 500ml/½ pint serving.*

A few days after the rock samphire scramble, Robin Nicholson divulged this, his grandmother's recipe; I'd obviously passed the test. If this recipe seems a little bit dated, that's because it is. It's at least 200 years old. We have no idea what 'the pickle should be so strong it carries an egg' means, but it sounds quaint. Robin tells us he used to eat it with boiled mutton during the war, but his favourite way to eat it it is with fish. He thinks, as we do, that it is better than capers in tartare sauce.

175g/6oz	SALT
1 litre	WATER
	YOUNG ROCK SAMPHIRE SHOOTS
2 handfuls	SAVOY (OR OTHER) CABBAGE LEAVES
500ml/½ pint	VINEGAR (APPROXIMATELY)
500ml/½	WATER (APPROXIMATELY)
	ROOT GINGER
	WHITE PEPPERCORNS
	CAYENNE PEPPER PODS

1. Boil the salt in the water, then cool.

2. Put the samphire in the salt water – 'The pickle should be so strong that it will carry an egg' – and leave until the samphire loses its colour, approximately two days.

3. Bring the mixture to the boil, boil for one minute, then take it off the heat and leave to go cold before draining.

4. Put some of the cabbage leaves in the bottom of a pan, then spoon the samphire on top. Cover with two or three more cabbage leaves.

5. Add vinegar and water, to cover, cover the pan with a lid and heat until boiling. The mixture will begin to go green. Keep at a constant heat for 15 minutes, then drain in a sieve, and dry with a cloth.

6. Put in glass jar, discarding the cabbage.

7. Boil some more vinegar, add a little root ginger, a handful of white peppercorns and some cayenne pepper pods.

8. Pour over the samphire, and cover when cool.

MARSH SAMPHIRE, OR GLASSWORT
{Salicornia europeae}

Sometimes known as sea asparagus, this is a prize among sea greens, if you can find it. Fishmongers used to give it away wrapped in paper with your weekly order of fish. The glossy green shoots are best steamed with melted butter.

IDENTIFICATION

FIND IT HERE:
Mudflats and estuaries around the country. Can be gathered from July onwards.
WHAT IT LOOKS LIKE:
Growing to about 2 metres (6 feet) high, plants are green and succulent. Each stem has pointed segmented spikes growing in pairs along it.

commonsense tips.

• Check that you are not in a national park or conservation area when you pick. Cut a few stems with a knife, leaving behind as much mud as possible!

• When cooking, the fleshy part strips off a thin woody stem.

STEAMED SAMPHIRE

Couple handfuls **SAMPHIRE STEMS PER PERSON**
250g/½lb **BUTTER, APPROXIMATELY, MELTED**

1. Wash the samphire well.

2. Cook the samphire, roots and all, in unsalted boiling water for 10 minutes.

3. Serve immediately with melted butter, or, alternatively, try it cold with Home-made Mayonnaise (see Page 133).

6 SEAWEED AND EAT IT

{Dulse, Carrageen, Laver, Sea Lettuce, Kelps}

SOLD ON SEAWEED

Date: *August 2003*

Andrew and Wei come to Britain to visit us on a delayed honeymoon, and we take them for a walk along the beach. As I wave my arms expansively, pointing out the stunning views over the Firth of Forth to the Pentland Hills beyond, Wei's eyes fix firmly on the seashore.

'Wow! Look at all that seaweed! Don't you eat it?' she says as she gazes at the acres of kelp anchored on the rocks at the low-tide mark, which, when submerged in water, looks like an enchanted forest.

I look at her as if she is crazy – until that moment, a walk on the beach was really about exercise, not about lunch – I didn't give the seaweed a second thought, other than being careful not to slip on it.

She, of course, is thinking the same about me – crazy Westerner – so out of touch with her natural surroundings that she doesn't even notice the abundance of readily available food growing in front of her eyes. A trip to the local Chinese supermarket reveals dried seaweed for sale in at least fifteen different forms: chopped sea lettuce to sprinkle on top of rice, seaweed soup, seaweed rolled into sheets, shredded seaweed, seaweed tied into knots to put into soup, vacuum-packed instant kelp, to name but a few – all imported all the way from China.

We decide to host a 'Hunter-Gatherer' weekend, where all the main ingredients are foraged from the beach or surroundings, to introduce our friends to the wonders of seaweed. Saturday morning, we give the men a task: to find some meat. Meanwhile, Xa and our friend Lulu are busy chatting and drinking coffee. I get antsy to be out – the sun is shining and I know my tide times. It's low tide. Time to go. 'Time and tide wait for no man!' I announce to the leisurely breakfasters, as the little girls and I head down to the beach, and start wading in the shallows for kelp and dulse. The ladies amble down, coffee cups in hand, and join in the seaweed hunt, and soon we have two carrier bags-full of dulse, collected from the stems of the oarweed, sea lettuce, and long fronds of green sugar kelp.

'Look what we've found!' The boys return, animated, in tune with their inner hunter-gatherer, with a bucketful of crab and one small lobster.

Later on, we invite the neighbours round for drinks, and serve them 'sea caper dip', a tapenade made with dulse. It all seems so normal, so civilised, this seaweed eating, we wonder what took us so long?

SEAWEED?

The British Isles, are, yes, islands, and surrounded by ... seaweed. If we delve into our past, the Scots and the Welsh and the Irish have cooked it up into soups, stews, puddings and breads for centuries. A Victorian amateur botanist, Reverend Allan McDonald, recorded, at the turn of the 20th century, over 40 Gaelic words for seaweed on the Western Isles, from '*bragaire*' to '*gleadhrach*' to '*totan*'.

But unlike Asian culture, where, for instance, the Japanese use some 21 species of seaweed in their everyday cooking, seaweed is not central to the British diet. Such is the inferiority complex of our native seaweeds that most references to seaweeds in the English language refer them by their Asian names, such as nori and wakame, instead of their native names, such as kelp, dulse, laver and sea lettuce.

Seaweed is not only tasty and abundant, it's the ultimate superfood. It is packed full of life-saving properties, rich in trace minerals such as potassium, iodine and magnesium. Asians have long understood this. Seaweed is used in Chinese herbal medicine as a cure for cancer, and, in 1974, a Japanese medical team planted cancerous tumours in mice, then fed them a diet of seaweed. Remarkably, the tumours disappeared. The Japanese also report that wakame, our sugarkelp, suppresses the re-absorption of cholesterol in the liver and intestine.

No seaweeds are poisonous, but introduce seaweed into your diet gradually, as, in some people, too much too soon can have a purgative effect.

Main British seaweeds and their other names:
- dulse – dillisk (*Palmaria palmate*)
- carrageen – Irish moss (*Chrondrus crispus*)
- sea lettuce (*Ulva lactuca*)
- laver – sloke – nori (*Porphyra umbilicalis*)
- kelp – oarweed – tangle – Kombu (*Laminaria digitata*)
- sugarwrack – sugarkelp (*Laminaria saccharina*)
- dabberlocks – wakame (*Alaria esculenta*)
- pepper dulse – (*Laurencia pinnatifida*)
- bladderwrack – fucus (*Fucus vesiculosus*)

HOW TO IDENTIFY, GATHER AND DRY SEAWEED

commonsense tips.

- You will need some plastic bags, your wellies (or nonslip shoes), a pair of scissors and a pen knife.

- Make sure that the beach is clean, and that there are no pipes bringing sewage or effluent anywhere near where you are searching.

- Cut the seaweed, don't pull it off. While seaweed doesn't have roots, it has the equivalent, a 'holdfast' that fixes the seaweed on to rocks or other seaweed, and, if you simply pull it off, it loses its ability to regenerate.

- Only gather small amounts for your own consumption. Commercial gathering of seaweed requires a licence.

- Gather seaweed 'in situ', as opposed to gathering the stuff that's washed up at the tide line. This might involve studying tide timetables to get out there at low tide, and might involved getting a bit wet, but it's worth it.

- Look at a tide timetable so you know when low tide is (tide timetables are usually available in the local newsagent or post office, or in the local paper, or on www.bbc.co.uk/weather/coast/tide). If you don't have a tide timetable, use your eyes, and remember that high tide is roughly one hour later each day, and low tide is six hours after high tide. To tell whether the tide is coming in or going out, you can put in a 'tide marker' at the tide line, then come back half an hour later to check whether it is submerged or dry.

STORE CUPBOARD

- All of the seaweeds listed above can be picked and then dried for later use. Seaweed can be stored for months.

- Rinse in fresh water to remove sand and sea life.

- Pick out some of the leaves that don't look so tasty.

- The seaweed can be soaked for a few hours to reduce the salt content, but it is not strictly necessary.

store cupboard

- Spread the seaweed out in the sun to dry, or on a towel or paper towel in a warm place, such as an airing cupboard, to dry naturally. Seaweed dries down to about one-fifth of its natural weight, so multiply by five when converting dried to fresh weight.
- Recipes that call for dry seaweed are assuming you don't have any fresh to hand – so, if you have fresh, you can use it.
- Dried seaweed should be soaked in fresh water before being used in any recipes.

DULSE
{Palmaria palmate}

If you are only going to try one seaweed, dulse is the one we would recommend; it has a distinctive flavour, (dubbed 'vegetarian oyster') and a lovely colour and texture. And it is distinctly ours, not called any other name and imported from Asia.

Dulse is our favourite seaweed for adding to cooked dishes, such as soups, stews and stir-fries, and we have added chopped raw dulse to salads to great effect and with no complaints from the family, who love it. Try dulse chopped into creamy mashed potato or into scrambled egg or a fish pie.

IDENTIFICATION
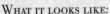

FIND IT HERE:
Dulse can be found year-round, but is best picked between May and October. It grows from a single holdfast, on its own in small clumps on rocks in the sand from the mid-shore, and down to the low tide mark, where it grows on the stems of larger kelps and oar weeds.

WHAT IT LOOKS LIKE:
It is dark brownish-red with purple tones, variable in size and shape. It may occur as a single broad or narrow blade, but is more likely to grow in several segments with rounded ends, and is delicate and thin.

WHAT CAN IT BE CONFUSED WITH?:
Red rag, which is a similar deep-red colour, but is much thicker and tougher. The fronds are roughly oval, although these oval shapes become 'ragged' as they get older and split with the wave action, and, unlike dulse, they are not fronds.

❧ CHEWING THE DULSE ❧

While their cows chew the cud, Irish dairy farmers chewed the dulse while milking them. Chewing strips of fresh dulse is rather like chewing on a salty rubber band, but, once dried, dulse changes in taste and texture; and, like olives, is an acquired taste. Coastal Irish and Highlanders chewed dried dulse as a savoury snack, and there are even records of dulse being sold on street corners in Boston when the first generation of Irish immigrants arrived in New England. Dulse was also sold on the streets of Edinburgh in post-Victorian times.

Using dulse for cooking has been around on these isles since at least 400 BC; however, the first recorded use of seaweed on these shores was around 600AD in a poem (sometimes attributed to St Columba), which mentions the dulse-gathering monks of Iona.

Coastal communities throughout the British Isles roasted dulse by rolling a hot poker on top of the seaweed until it bubbled and crackled.

SEA-CAPER DIP *Makes one large jar.*

We served this dip to some unsuspecting neighbours who came over for a drink, not realising we were playing out a hunter-gatherer weekend, where all the key ingredients had to be foraged. It was the first seaweed-inspired dish we served, spread on oatcakes, washed down with a cold jug of Pimms. The ladies polished it off – all the feedback we needed!

OLIVES (PITTED OLIVES FROM JAR ARE FINE)
CAPERS
GARLIC CLOVES, CRUSHED
DULSE, FRESH OR DRIED
EXTRA-VIRGIN OLIVE OIL
LEMON
SEA SALT AND FRESHLY GROUND BLACK PEPPER

1. Using two parts olives to one part capers, put all the ingredients, apart from the salt and pepper, into a food processor and whiz it around for just a few seconds, so that the dip is blended but not pureed.

2. Season to taste, then serve with mini-oatcakes or bread-sticks.

commonsense tips.

Once dried, dulse can be stored indefinitely in air-tight containers or plastic bags. It rehydrates to its original size and texture after a few minutes in water. Dulse doesn't dry crisp and brittle as other seaweeds, but remains soft and pliable, and it can be pressed together and stored fresh in the fridge for at least a month.

SEA HARVEST SOUP *Makes 6 servings.*

This is a perfect warming winter dish. The dulse has a high mineral content and adds an interesting salty, iodine note to this vegetable soup. You can use dried seaweed, but you need less of it. If you want it to be thicker still, on those freezing, wind battered evenings, we suggest adding a handful of lentils with the potatoes.

30g/1oz	BUTTER
1 tbsp	OLIVE OIL
200g/7oz	FRESHLY PICKED DULSE, CAREFULLY WASHED AND CHOPPED
1 clove	GARLIC, CRUSHED
1	ONION, FINELY CHOPPED
2	LEEKS, WHITE AND LIGHT GREEN PARTS ONLY, FINELY CHOPPED
4 medium-sized	POTATOES, PEELED AND DICED
500ml/½ pint	OF VEGETABLE STOCK
500ml/½ pint	WATER
Juice of ½	LEMON
5floz/¼ pint	MILK TO THIN SOUP (OPTIONAL)
	SALT AND COARSELY GROUND BLACK PEPPER
1 handful	CHOPPED PARSLEY

1. Heat the butter and oil in a medium sized pan. Sweat the dulse, garlic, onion and leeks until beginning to colour and soften.

2. Add potatoes to pan. Pour in stock and water until the vegetables are covered.

3. Cook over a medium heat for approximately ten minutes, until potatoes are soft.

4. Remove from heat and liquidise in food processor. Add squeeze of lemon juice and add milk to required consistency.

5. Season with salt and pepper and throw in the chopped parsley. Serve with hunks of bread or oatcakes.

FRENCH ONION SOUP WITH DULSE *Makes 6 servings.*

The usual wholesome broth, but with a little twist that will nourish you and get you back on your feet.

1–2 tbsp	EXTRA-VIRGIN OLIVE OIL
4 medium	ONIONS, CUT INTO SLICES
1 large handful	DULSE, SOAKED IN WATER AND FINELY CHOPPED
1 glass	WHITE WINE
1.5 litres / 2½ pints	GOOD CHICKEN OR MEAT STOCK
	SEA SALT AND FRESHLY GROUND BLACK PEPPER
150g/5oz	GRUYÈRE CHEESE, GRATED
1	BAGUETTE, SLICED AND TOASTED

1. Heat the oil in a soup pan and sauté the onions over a medium heat, until soft but not brown, turning with a wooden spoon.

2. While the onions are cooking, add the dulse.

3. Add the wine, and boil until the liquid has almost disappeared, then gradually add the stock.

4. Now add the salt and pepper, cover and simmer over a low heat for 20 minutes.

5. Meanwhile, sprinkle the Gruyère on the toasted baguette slices, and grill until the cheese melts.

6. When ready to serve, float the cheesy-toast slices in the hot soup.

GREEN SALAD WITH DULSE AND WALNUTS

Makes 4 servings.

This salad uses either fresh or dried dulse, with the seaweed combining well with the hot bite of the rocket. Sunflower or pumpkin seeds, or other nuts such as toasted almonds, would also work well with this dish, if you don't have walnuts to hand.

1 cup	FRESH DULSE, FINELY CHOPPED, OR ½ cup DRIED DULSE FLAKES
4 large handfuls	ROCKET, OR OTHER SALAD GREENS, INCLUDING WILD GREENS SUCH AS DANDELION AND SORREL
4 tbsp	EXTRA-VIRGIN OLIVE OIL
	SEA SALT
4 tbsp	LEMON JUICE
	FRESHLY GROUND BLACK PEPPER
½ cup	ROASTED WALNUT HALVES

1. If using fresh dulse, pick over the fronds and check for sand or small shells, then rinse and pat dry, chop finely and put into a salad bowl.

2. Add the greens, and toss with olive oil and salt.

3. Add the lemon juice and black pepper.

4. Garnish with the walnuts.

IRISH GRANNY'S BROWN SODA BREAD WITH DULSE

My Irish mother-in-law used to make soda bread daily, which she ate spread generously with butter and honey while drinking endless cups of tea. Somehow, despite eating artery-clogging amounts of butter, she was eternally slim. The unique taste of soda bread always reminds me of her, and, although she died before we started collecting seaweed and adding it to recipes, I know she would have approved.

225g/8oz	WHITE FLOUR
1 heaped tsp	BICARBONATE OF SODA
1 pinch	SEA SALT
115g/4oz	SOFT MARGARINE
225g/8oz	COARSE-GROUND WHOLEMEAL FLOUR
15g/½oz (small handful)	DRIED DULSE, SOAKED IN WATER FOR 5 MINUTES AND FINELY CHOPPED

400ml/14fl oz **BUTTERMILK OR SOURED CREAM**

1. Sieve the white flour, soda and salt into a bowl.

2. Rub in the margarine.

3. Add the wholemeal flour and dulse, then pour in the buttermilk, mixing continually.

4. Bake in a preheated oven at 400°F/200°C/Gas 6, for 30–45 minutes. If the top of the bread gets too brown before the end of cooking, put some foil on top of it.

COOKING WITH SEAWEED

My first experience of seaweed wasn't a success. Simon and I cooked laver bread with lamb, as the final test on our friend Adrian Gill's cooking course. We'd covered the full spectrum of offal and squeamish bits, including brain and pigs trotters. This was the meal on which our cooking talents (or lack of) hung.

It wasn't a great hit, not because of the way we had cooked it, but because we weren't sure about the taste combination. We had a good evening anyway, and Adrian passed us, mainly because we had managed to find a tin of laver bread at a time when, outside of the Chinese restaurant culture, seaweed lived firmly on the beach.

Around this time, I also tried carrageen. I bought a pouch-full in the Outer Hebrides, in a gift shop, where it was sitting alongside scarves and Harris wool socks, and made it into a vanilla pudding, along with wild strawberries and double cream. I loved the taste, carrying a faint whiff of the sea, and vowed that next time I cooked it, I would pick the seaweed off the beach myself.

This was only the beginning of my taste experience being pushed into unknown areas, before I realised that seaweeds are as varied as vegetables from your grocer's shop – dulse is rich and meaty, while carrageen carries a delicate smell of the waves.

A friend who is a trained cook informed me with passion, 'I don't like eating seaweed,' which is like saying, 'I don't eat vegetables.' We plan to invite her to dinner and wind dulse into a dish and wait until she asks for seconds. I feel certain that she will succumb.

CARRAGEEN OR IRISH MOSS
{Chondrus crispus}

Carrageen is nature's pudding maker, a natural gelatine, full of healthful properties, and imparts its own flavour to a variety of savoury and sweet ingredients, for a variety of tastes.

Savoury mousses can be made with shrimps, tomato or cucumber, while the sweet mousse can be flavoured with anything from chocolate to vanilla to fruit juice. Our personal favourite is the vanilla milk pudding with drizzled rosehip syrup, made in individual moulds and turned out. Most kids love jelly, and making their favourite party food with carrageen is a real novelty.

IDENTIFICATION

FIND IT HERE:
Carrageen is found on rocky shores at low tide, on the middle or lower shore in and around rock pools. It is usually found growing beneath the kelp.

WHAT IT LOOKS LIKE:
Dark red to pink, but can have green blotches. Fan-shaped with small spiked fronds leading off each spoke. Grows more luxuriantly in calmer waters.

WHAT CAN IT BE CONFUSED WITH?:
Batter frond, a dark brownish-red plant that is less varied in form and colour. Unlike carrageen, there are often small, boil-like fruits at the end of the fronds.

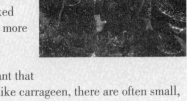

commonsense tips.

Carrageen is, traditionally, bleached and dried, until it is creamy or pinkish white. However, if you plan to use it immediately, there is no reason to go through the bleaching and drying process; the only reason to do so is that it stores better this way.

We picked the carrageen, took it home, rinsed it, then laid it out on sunny stone steps. Luckily, the weather was showery, and we watched it turn from brown to dark purple to light purple to pinkish creamy white, and when it was dry, stored it in an old cotton pillowcase.

However, if you don't have the time or the inclination to go through the bleaching process, simply rinse the carrageen and put it somewhere warm to dry before storing it.

❧ QUEEN OF CARRAGEEN ❧

Margaret Horn grew up in the fishing village of Auchmithie, on the north-east coast of Scotland. Today, she runs a restaurant, But'n' Ben, there, with her son, Angus. Now in her seventies, she doesn't look at day over 55, which we can only attribute to her seaweed eating!

'I walk along the beach most days with my dogs and eat dulse as I go. I'm still here to tell the tale. As a child, seaweed was a large part of our diet, and it was the same for all the fisher folk. I remember my mother and grandmother making big bowls of carrageen pudding, which we ate most nights for supper. We also roasted the dulse: we would heat the poker and run it over the top of the dulse, and the dulse would crinkle up. The flavour is delicious and was a family favourite. Dulse and potato soup was a popular dish in the village. We supplemented this diet with buckies (the local name for winkles), wee treats, as we thought of them, and partons (crabs). At the But'n' Ben, we incorporate seaweed into the menu on a daily basis. Dulse goes on our seafood platter and we usually have carrageen pudding on the menu, sweetened with a bit of sugar and served with a fruit purée and cream.

'I like my carrageen pudding just plain, because I like the taste of the sea. I could sup carrageen till the cows come home.'

CARRAGEEN PUDDING *Makes 6–8 servings.*

750ml/26fl oz **MILK**
10g/1/3oz **CARRAGEEN (DRIED OR, IF IN SEASON, FRESH)**
Juice 2 **ORANGES**
1 **VANILLA POD (SEEDS SCRAPED OUT AND THROWN AWAY)**
Rind ½ **LEMON**
2 tsp **CASTER SUGAR**

1. Heat the milk until almost to boiling point, then add the other ingredients.

2. Keep on the heat and stir until it begins to thicken (approximately 10 minutes). The longer you simmer it for, the more solid it will set.

3. Strain through a fine sieve and allow to cool and set, then serve in individual glasses or in a bowl.

CARRAGEEN AND CINNAMON ICE CREAM

This recipe comes from LoTide Fine Foods (www.lo-tide.com) , an Irish company that specialises in providing sea vegetables.

15g/½oz (handful) **CARRAGEEN**
500ml/1 pint **CREAM**
500ml/1 pint **PINT MILK**
1 **CINNAMON STICK, CHOPPED**
HONEY, TO TASTE

1. Soak the carrageen , until pliable, about 15–20 minutes.

2. Drain and put into a saucepan, together with the milk, cream and cinnamon, then bring to the boil and simmer for 15–20 minutes.

3. Strain the milk, and allow to cool.

4. Add honey to taste, then freeze in an ice-cream maker as per the manufacturer's instructions, or follow the steps for Lyn's Lavender Ice Cream (see Page 74).

STRAWBERRY AND RASPBERRY JELLY

Makes 4 servings.

310ml/11fl oz FRUIT JUICE
14g/½oz CARRAGEEN
225g/8oz STRAWBERRIES, WASHED AND CUT INTO HALVES
125g/4oz RASPBERRIES, WASHED
1 tbsp ORANGE RIND, GRATED
MAPLE SYRUP OR HONEY, TO TASTE

1. Place the fruit juice and carrageen into a pan, bring to a boil and gently simmer for 10–15 minutes.

2. Add the strawberries, raspberries and grated orange rind, and the syrup or honey, to taste, and gently mix together all the ingredients.

3. Place the mixture in a glass serving bowl, leave to cool until set, then garnish and serve.

CARRAGEEN FOR YOUR HEALTH

Carrageen has long been used to make tasty and easily digested puddings for children and the ailing, and Algin, a commercial product derived from carrageen, is used to make chocolate milk and ice cream. Carrageen pudding with jam is a staple in the Victorian nursery puddings. The doyenne of all things domestic, Mrs Beeton, gives recipes using carrageen in her chapter on 'Invalid Cooking', along with recipes for Beef Tea, Chicken Soup and Blackcurrant Tea. So, next time someone you love is ailing, fix them up with carrageen.

LAVER (OR SLOKE, OR NORI)
{Porphyra umbiliculis}

IDENTIFICATION

FIND IT HERE:
Laver grows in similar places to carrageen , on rocks and stones, especially on rugged shores on the West Coast. It grows at all tide levels from March through to autumn. Gather it from shallow rock pools at low tide in April and May, and through the summer.

WHAT IT LOOKS LIKE:
Laver looks like a darker version of sea lettuce; it has purply brown-green, almost translucent sheets or leaves.

HOW TO PICK:
Gently pick the sheets of laver off the rocks, then wash it carefully in sea-water until it is clean. Spread out to dry in the sun or in a warm, dry place, or cook it into laver bread.

COOKING WITH LAVER

Welsh chefs use laver bread in recipes with lamb, and it is a traditional British and Irish breakfast food, cooked with bacon fat and oats. We have tried cooking with laver, and find the taste rather too bitter for our liking – but try it for yourselves.

TRADITIONAL LAVER BREAD BREAKFAST

LAVER BREAD (SEE NEXT PAGE)
ROLLED OATS
EXTRA-VIRGIN OLIVE OIL (OR BACON FAT)

1. Put the laverbread into a bowl, add rolled oats, and mix together thoroughly.

2. Divide the mixture into small cakes, then fry them in a pan with the olive oil or bacon fat.

LAVER BREAD

'Bread' is probably not the best description for this concoction, but that is the word the Welsh use for this traditional way of cooking laver. Most recipes that use laver are describing laver that is cooked in this way.

LAVER
WATER
SEA SALT (OR BICARBONATE OF SODA)

1. Wash the seaweed thoroughly, so that it's clean of sand. You may have to run it under the water several times.

2. Soak it for a few hours with a little salt or bicarbonate of soda, to get rid of some of the bitterness.

3. Drain, then transfer it to a thick-bottomed pan, cover with fresh water, and simmer until it turns to jelly; this could take several hours!

4. When it is cool, it can be stored for 2–3 weeks in a plastic container in the fridge.

SEA LETTUCE
{*Ulva lactuca*}

commonsense tips.

• Cut the less ragged darker membranes with scissors, leaving the holdfast, or root.

• Rinse the sea lettuce under a cold tap, removing any sea life or sand. Use a salad spinner to remove moisture, or squeeze the water out with your hands.

• Sea lettuce is great for cooking 'en papillote'; as a wrap for any fish you are grilling, poaching, or baking. We used it for our kebabs and were amazed how juicy the scallops stayed as a result, while the sea lettuce is a delicious, crispy wrapper.

• Sea lettuce (like all seaweeds) can be eaten raw or dried. It is a delicious addition to soups, stews and rice.

IDENTIFICATION

FIND IT HERE:
Best gathered at low tide, sea lettuce grows near rocks or on the stems of larger seaweeds, and prefers beaches with a fresh-water outlet somewhere.
WHAT IT LOOKS LIKE:
It has bright green tissue-papery leaves. Sea lettuce is sometimes called 'green laver', as it looks similar to laver.

SCALLOP KEBABS WITH SEA LETTUCE WRAP

Makes 6–8 servings.

	SEA LETTUCE (1 LARGE PIECE SHOULD BE ENOUGH TO WRAP 1 SCALLOP)
32	KING SCALLOPS (WITH THE CORAL REMOVED)
16	WOODEN SKEWERS
32	CHERRY TOMATOES
2	FENNEL BULBS, BAKED FOR 10 MINUTES IN A HOT OVEN (400°F/200°C/GAS 6), TO SOFTEN, THEN QUARTERED
Packet	OF PANCETTA
	OIL TO BRUSH KEBABS
2	LEMONS, QUARTERED

1. Individually wrap each scallop in a large piece of sea lettuce. Keep the parcel knitted together with the wooden skewer.

2. Alternate scallops with cherry tomatoes, fennel and rolled-up pancetta on each stick; about six chunks, including at least two scallops, on each skewer, allowing two kebabs per person.

3. Place the kebabs on the barbecue, turning regularly and making sure the sea lettuce crisps without burning, approximately 5 to 10 minutes cooking.

4. Serve with a plate of rice, couscous or bulgur wheat, and the lemon to squeeze over the scallops to taste.

KELPS (OR KOMBU)

Kelps are a staple of Asian cuisine, forming the basis of most soups and noodle dishes – including miso soup – and once their secrets have been unlocked, cooking with them is really very simple. We use the term 'kelp' to describe all three seaweeds in our recipes.

IDENTIFICATION

Laminaria saccharina (Sugarwrack)
FIND IT HERE:
Kelps will only be exposed at low tides, and collecting them may involve getting wet, but that's half the fun. It grows in rock pools and on stones and rocks.
WHAT IT LOOKS LIKE:
Laminaria saccharina (sugarwrack), as the name suggests, is a sweet tasting seaweed, deriving its sweetness from a

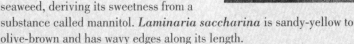

substance called mannitol. *Laminaria saccharina* is sandy-yellow to olive-brown and has wavy edges along its length.

Laminaria digitata (oarweed)
FIND IT HERE:
Laminaria digitata (oarweed or tangle) are the large seaweed 'trees' that grow at or below the low tide line. They anchor onto rocks and are only exposed at low tide.
WHAT IT LOOKS LIKE:
Laminaria digitata has big, shiny, leathery olive-brown thongs.

Alaria esculenta (dabberlocks, babberlocks)
FIND IT HERE:
On the lower shore on exposed rocks.
WHAT IT LOOKS LIKE:
Alaria esculenta is a gold–brown winged kelp that has a narrow midrib along the entire length of its blade. When dried, its colour varies between a very dark green to almost black.

COMMONSENSE TIPS

• All kelps are best be harvested in springtime, when the new shoots are young. The edible part of dabberlocks can grow to a considerable length, but for the best quality, pick when it is younger and generally smaller, between March and June, when it is bright green.

• When harvested, the kelps can be cut into ribbons, or shredded, and dried.

• Kelps should be dried very quickly – within 24 hours.

• The young kelps can grow 2–3 feet in the springtime, but, when collecting, leave the holdfast intact, so it can regenerate.

COOKING WITH KELPS

Kelp gathered from our shores in springtime, and dried for later use, can form the basis of nourishing broths and noodle dishes. The main secret is a broth made from cooking the kelp with shiitake mushrooms, which is then combined with miso.

Kelp can also be shredded or chopped into 2-centimetre (1/2-inch) pieces and added to stir-fries and soups.

Kelp is a great vegetarian food, especially good for adding to bean recipes, as the properties of the kelp help to break down the fibre in the beans, thus reducing on flatulence!

NOODLES AND VEGETABLES IN BROTH *Makes 4–6 servings.*

Asians are great at tasty, flavoursome fast food. This is the Asian equivalent of the lunchtime sandwich, and much more satisfying.

2 packets	UDON OR SOBA NOODLES
	SELECTION GREEN VEGETABLES (SUCH AS BROCCOLI, SPINACH, NETTLES, GREEN BEANS)
1.5–2 litres	OF DASHI STOCK (SEE PAGE 117)
1 pinch	SEA SALT
4 tbsp	SOY SAUCE
3 tbsp	MIRIN
3–4 tsp	JUICE FRESHLY GRATED GINGER ROOT
	SPRING ONIONS, CHOPPED

1. Cook the noodles according to the directions on the packet, then rinse under cold running water, drain, and set aside.

2. Steam the green vegetables, and set aside.

3. Meanwhile, combine the dashi stock, salt, soy sauce and mirin, simmer for one minute, then remove from the heat and add the ginger juice.

4. Divide the noodles between individual deep bowls, and ladle the hot broth over each to almost cover.

5. Top with the steamed vegetables, and garnish with the spring onions.

WHITE MISO AND WAKAME SOUP *Makes 4 servings.*

1 piece WAKAME (*Alaria esculenta*), 30CM/12IN LONG
1.5 litres/2½ pints DASHI, VEGETABLE STOCK OR WATER
1 large or 2 medium CARROTS, SLICED THINLY
6 small SPRING ONIONS, CUT INTO 1CM/½IN PIECES
80g/3oz WHITE MISO

1. Soak the wakame for 10 minutes (if dried), cut away any tough ribs, then slice the fronds into two centimetre (one inch) pieces.

2. Meanwhile, pour the dashi into a saucepan and bring to the boil, then add the carrots and simmer for 10 minutes.

3. Next, add the spring onions and simmer for a few more minutes, then add the wakame to the soup, simmer for 2 minutes, then remove from the heat.

4. In a cup, thin the miso with a little bit of the hot soup, then add this liquid back to the pan, stirring the miso into the soup. Leave for a couple of minutes so that the flavours can mingle.

DASHI STOCK FOR ASIAN SOUPS *Makes 4 servings.*

The main ingredient of Asian broths, including miso soup, is dashi, a stock made from kelp.

2 pieces KOMBU (ANY OF THE KELPS), 15cm/6in long
3 DRIED SHIITAKE MUSHROOMS
2 litres WATER

1. In a saucepan, soak the kombu (if dried) and the mushrooms in the water for at least 15 minutes.

2. Remove the mushrooms, and thinly slice the caps.

3. Return the mushrooms to the pan, bring it to the boil and simmer gently for 10 minutes.

4. Remove the kombu and keep it to use for cooking as a condiment or with beans.

SEAWEED FOR YOUR HEALTH

The Chinese use seaweed in all kinds of treatments for disorders involving swelling, fluid retention, tumours and lymphatic drainage.

According to Chinese medicine, the properties in kelps enter the channels of the liver, stomach and kidneys, and they use kelps to treat edema, tumours and gout and testicular pain and swelling.

Laver (***Porphyra umbiliculis***) affects the channel of the lungs, and is used by Chinese doctors to treat beriberi (leg swelling), edema, urinary infections, gout and sore throats.

SEAWEED IS SLIMMING!

A number of 'anti-fat' seaweed-based slimming aids were sold in the 19th century; for example, bladderwrack tea (bladderwrack is the seaweed that has air bubbles on its stems, which you can pop a bit like bubblewrap).

There may have been something in it: seaweeds contain high levels of iodine, which is necessary for the proper functioning of the thyroid gland; and a more active thyroid makes you burn calories faster.

❧❦EAT SEAWEED AND SURVIVE NUCLEAR FALLOUT!❦❧

The Japanese have long believed that eating seaweed helps to protect against the effects of radiation exposure. This is because a substance found in seaweed, sodium alginate, binds with radioactive strontium, and eliminates it from the body. Accordingly, it is touted as a way of countering the side effects of radiotherapy treatment in cancer sufferers.

The Japanese also report that wakame (*Alaria esculenta*) suppresses the re-absorbtion of cholesterol in the liver and intestine.

At the time of the atomic bombing of Nagasaki in 1945, most patients at the St Francis Hospital in Nagasaki, who had been located one mile from the centre of the blast, survived the initial effects of the bomb, but soon after came down with symptoms of radiation sickness from the radioactivity that had been released. A doctor at the hospital, Tatsuichiro Akizuki, MD, fed his staff a strict macrobiotic diet of brown rice, miso and tamari soy soup, wakame and other sea vegetables, Hokkaaido pumpkin, and sea salt, and prohibited the consumption of sugar and sweets. None of his staff came down with radiation sickness.

❧❦SEAWEED AS THE ANSWER TO GLOBAL WARMING❦❧

Seaweed has so much going for it. Not only is it the cure for all kinds of ailments, it might also help in the fight against global warming.

Seaweed absorbs greenhouse gases, trapping carbon dioxide, and converts it back into oxygen. The fast-growing seaweeds, **Sargassum** and **Sostera marina**, grow around 40 feet a year. Scientists at the Mitsubishi Research Institute and Tokyo University have hatched a plan for a giant seaweed plantation in the sea off the coast of Japan – 100 vast nets full of the seaweeds, over an area 9.5 kilometres (6 miles) square.

After a year of growth, the seaweed will be harvested to turn into biofuel. The harvested seaweed is blasted with superheated steam; it then discharges hydrogen and carbon monoxide, to produce a biofuel that doesn't emit any carbon dioxide.

A SEASIDE FORAGING CHALLENGE

Date: *Mid-May*

Place: *Beach and woodland*

Objective: *To convert the sceptical*

We decide to find some 'forage virgins' to try out some of our newfound skills and recipes on; some typical urban-dwellers for whom foraging is what you can find in the back of a fridge.

Mid-May, Saturday, 12.30 p.m.

Claire and Frazer McCready and their three children, Campbell, Jack and Charlie, arrive from Glasgow, and are feeling nervous. Claire arrives with a huge bag of chocolate mini-eggs. 'We stocked up on bacon sandwiches at breakfast,' says Claire. 'And we stopped at McDonald's,' she adds.

Lydia and her friend Coralie have jumped the gun: they arrived in the garden earlier in the morning after a trip to the beach, pleased with their prize specimens of dulse and oarweed.

2 p.m.

We rally the troops and assemble in the garden for a team photo. We divide the foragers into two teams, and we each have a list of about 10 items that we may or may not find. We agree to reconvene at 5 p.m. to compare scores.

Team A (Xa's team) – adults: Xa, Frazer, Louisa; children: Adair, Campbell, Jack, Geordie and Finnian.

Team B (Fiona's team) – adults: Fiona, Claire, Miles; children: Charlie, Lydia, Coralie and Perdie.

Claire pulls her baseball cap on firmly and zips up her coat. 'Right, Frazer, we're not going to be townies!' she says, with grim determination.

Team A

We're ready, bags in hand, with everything to play for. The tide is right. It's miles out and we can approach the seaweed line with confidence. Frazer is looking nervous – a surfboard might be a more acceptable appendage than a crumpled bag.

We cut some dark red glossy pieces of dulse from a tangled mass of kelp anchored on the seabed.

We move further on and notice the boys forming a huddle in the sand.

They are digging with a forgotten pink spade, more forage of the nonedible kind.

We spy a patch of mint growing near the sand where the boys are digging. 'Oi, come and smell this leaf!' I wave at Geordie, and he comes over dragging his spade.

'Mint,' he says, wearily. He's done with foraging and the tide is coming in.

As we near the beach bungalows, we see a small pointed leaf edging through the shingle. Louisa is checking the shape of the leaf against the identification book in her hand.

'Orache!' Frazer exclaims, looking over her shoulder.

I can see our stir-fry with prawns is taking shape. We stagger down the beach, totting up our edible trophies and it is still only four o'clock.

Team B

We head off to the nearby woods. Our list includes some late spring greens, watercress, sorrel, elderflower and whatever else we can find.

We pass by a wild gooseberry bush – I make a mental note to come back later in the year.

We pick some jack-by-the-hedge, or hedge garlic. I have the gloves, so I'm on nettle heads. It's getting late in the season for prime spring greens, but we are in the woods here, so, in shady spots, the spring greens are just worth picking.

Charlie's collection of sticks is getting larger by the minute. Claire is gradually warming to the expedition as Charlie's enthusiasm grows in line with his stick collection, and we pick some sweet-smelling elderflower heads – just out, these would be good in a crumble, if only we had some rhubarb.

I give Claire a sorrel leaf to munch on. 'You're joking!' she exclaims, as she asks me to take her picture. 'This will give me something to talk about in the playground!' she continues, as she bites into the leaf.

On the way home, we see some mushrooms called Jew's Ears, which we know are good in soups and stir-fries, and a bracket mushroom called Dryad's saddle, which, although it looks a bit old and dried out, we think will still count. Our protein possibilities are improving.

5.00 p.m.

Xa's team are already home and they're feeling cocky because they've found stuff that wasn't on their list. However, they haven't seen yet what we have in our bags. We disgorge the bags and do a tally. Fifteen edibles.

Team A: sea lettuce, dulse, rhubarb, fennel, Alexanders, orache, (plus inedibles: beach ball, pink spade, shells).

Team B: Jack-by-the-hedge, nettles, Jew's Ear, watercress, sorrel, elderflower, ground ivy, (plus inedibles: bird's nest made from feathers, wild flowers, sticks and stones).

We decide to call it a draw.

Next, the menu: A soufflé of spring greens. Quick and easy, it will give our guests a moment of drama; they are looking happy but in need of a food fix. We combine the oraches and dulse in a stir-fry with rice and prawns, the sea lettuce wraps round the scallops to make kebabs, and the 'wild' rhubarb will meld with the elderflower as a natural sweetener.

9 p.m.
The verdict.

'I thought I was going to have to eat things I didn't want to eat,' says Claire as she polishes off her kebab, and the dulse and orache stir-fried rice, 'but that's actually nice.' It's all starting to come naturally to her.

There's not a scrap of seaweed left on her plate.

'I thoroughly enjoyed myself today,' she admits. 'I didn't think the boys would buy into it, but they did. That made a big difference.'

Job done. Time to relax and enjoy a glass or two of wine.

⚘ LATE SPRING SUPPER BY THE SEASHORE ⚘

Wild Greens Soufflé
*
Sea Lettuce-wrapped Scallop Kebabs

Stir-fried Rice with Dulse and Orache
*
Rhubarb and Elderflower Crumble

7 UTTERLY SHELLFISH

{ Cockles, Crab, Lobster, Shrimps & Prawns, Moluscs, Whelks, Winkles }

LONGING FOR LOBSTERS

Place: *East coast of Scotland*

Date: *5 August*

Objective: *Sunday lunch*

8 a.m.

The boat-owning summer residents of this fishing village are out trawling for mackerel and checking lobster pots, before the rest of the leisurely Sunday-paper readers are up and before the tide turns.

Our plan for later in the day, at low tide, is to catch lobsters, crabs and other beach edibles by digging them out of their rocky hiding places by hand with the aid of long-handled hooks. We fancy ourselves purists, 'foragers of the people', on a quest to prove you can do it the hard way; but actually, we don't have any choice, as we have neither a lobster pot, nor a boat.

The chat around the harbour wall is all about how many lobsters there are out there for Sunday lunch. Mr Hotshot Lawyer and his wife have just come back from checking their pots. 'We got four lobsters yesterday: three in one pot, one in the other,' he says. But now we know the lobsters are out there, we feel confident that we too can catch them.

12 p.m.

It's low tide, and we assemble on the beach armed with all sorts of lobstering gadgets.

Our prize forager, we hope, is William Milliken, the author of the book, Flora Celtica, and a botanist of international renown. We have managed to track him down and invite him on our lobstering expedition.

Will turns out to be about six feet six inches tall, slim, gentle and extremely handsome, and is armed not only with a home-made lobster hook, but with tales of foraging in Norwegian fjords and derring-do in the Peruvian desert. Things are looking up.

The children have all kinds of improvised catching devices, from shrimp nets to old plastic tubs. Our lobster hooker is a handle of a paint-roller screwed on to an old broom handle. Jeremy arrives with a window-opening pole.

'Did you know that a lobster pincer is strong enough to cut your finger off?' says Jeremy. Suddenly, gardening gloves seem woefully inadequate, as we look at his elbow-length thick rubber gloves.

12.30 p.m.

The beaches are deserted – everyone else is having Sunday lunch.

We head off down to the far end of the bay, where the outgoing tide has exposed strata of seaweed-covered rocks, littered with the type of pools and holes beloved of the lobster.

'Look, lobster, over here!' shouts Duncan. We turn round, excited, only to find Duncan has pulled a lobster pot out of the water. We resist the temptation to raid the lobster pot; there has to be some moral code to seashore foraging.

At the far end of the bay, where the gently sloping strata form a small cliff face, we start finding some crabs. Each time we lift the tasselled curtain of seaweed, there is a crab nestled behind. Some are the aptly named, reddish-brown-coloured, brown edible crab (**Cancer pagurus**), others are the dark-green/brown-coloured shore crabs, both of which are edible, if a bit small to feed all of us.

1 p.m.

William is in his element – he's on to seaweed; he's more comfortable with plants than creatures, and the plants are far less elusive.

'Here, pepper dulse!' William is holding up a small piece of seaweed the size of a pinky. It has tiny fern-like fronds, and looks nothing like the larger dulse.

'Try this!' he urges, handing a bunch over. Knowing the water is clean round here, we grab the tiny frond and put it in our mouths, not knowing what to expect.

Mmmmm, interesting, peppery and unusual and …yes, we would definitely eat this again. William has now earned his lunch.

Will dips down into the water and comes back with an edible sea urchin. They are quite hard to find, because they live below the low tide mark, so this is quite a find.

The children start to get hungry. Pity, because Jeremy and Duncan have just found a pool of shrimps and are closing in on an area of rocks where we spotted a lobster being caught last summer:

One last push

As Xa and the kids retreat, we head for the last rocky pool. I let Jeremy and Duncan take the lead – and play out their hunter-gatherer instinct, going in for the kill. We lift up the seaweed and poke the hook into the back of a crevice, and hook a small lobster into the waiting bucket.

2 p.m.

It's late. Back along the headland with Will, we're famished now. We find some scurvy grass, beloved of scurvy-suffering seashore dwellers for its vitamin C content. 'I put this in my salads,' William tells us. We gather some to add zest to our salad, and a bag full of lovage. William also finds some wild thyme for the final flavouring for our lunch.

It's not quite a lobster feast, but along with the crabs and the other molluscs we have collected, as well as the seaweeds, sea urchin and sea greens, we are confident we can rustle something up.

Lunch, 2.30 p.m.

The men set about washing, chopping, cleaning and gathering the edibles we've found. The lobster, crabs, whelks and winkles, pepper dulse, sea lettuce and some lovage and wild thyme all go in a pot, covered with water, to be cooked up into a seashore bisque.

We split open the sea urchin with a hammer, and look at the innards and decide it is somewhere between taramasalata and houmous. We scoop the roe out and put it in a bowl.

The menu reveals itself, gradually. We start off with the onion and dulse soup and hunks of crusty bread – a big hit with the children. Then we move on to Grilled Mackerel with Gooseberry Sauce (see Page 136). The tart sauce complements the fish beautifully. The children pronounce themselves full, and run off to play.

The adults move on to urchin roe with oatcakes, and the green salad with the wild greens.

Next it's the Seashore Bisque (see Page 135–6), made from the crabs, the lobster, and the other shellfish we've collected.

Yes, you may need lobster pots for a purely lobster feast, but, we persuade ourselves, our cobbled-together feast is far more interesting.

LOBSTERS

WHEN:

June to November

FIND IT HERE:

Lobsters live in rocky crevices in deep water. The best hunting grounds for lobster (and crabs) are in the shallow waters below the tidal zone and in the tidal pools. These crevices are often covered with seaweed.

LEGAL SIZE:

0.5k/1lb (it takes 5–7 years for a lobster to grow to legal size in the ocean); body 9cm/3½in.

HOW OLD CAN LIVE TO?:

100 years old. Fifteen years or more is typical, though.

HOW BIG DO THEY GROW?:

3 feet or more in overall length.

COMMONSENSE TIPS

CATCHING THEM WITH POTS:

1. You do not need a licence to put out a lobster pot, provided the lobsters and crabs you catch are for your own consumption.
2. Remember that fishermen make their livings this way, be sensitive to where they fish and where they have laid down their pots.
3. If you do not have a boat, you can throw out a lobster pot at low tide off the rocks. Lobster pots need to be baited, usually with fish bait: the off-cuts from processing fish, such as the heads or skeletons.

CATCHING THEM BY HAND:

1. **TOOLS:** A long pole with a hook on the end to prise the lobster out of its hiding place, as well as a good pair of gloves and a bucket or bag to put the lobster in.
2. **STRATEGY:** This is a hard way of catching lobster (and crabs); the success rate is not as high as with baited pots, but it is a whole load of fun. Establish where the lobsters like to hang out, to increase your chances. Wait for low tide, and wade out to exposed rock pools, lift up the seaweed curtain and hopefully hook out the lobster.

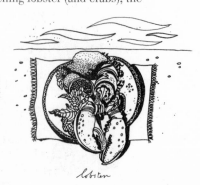

lobster

CRABS

WHEN:
Mid-April through to November.

WHAT:
The two main types of crab found throughout the British Isles are the brown edible crab and the shore crab, which are perfectly flavoursome. Other crabs that can be caught are the spider crabs, though only in the warmer southern waters, and the velvet swimming crabs, wich tend to live below the low tide mark, but may turn up in pots or occasionally on a baited crab line.

WHEN IS A CRAB TOO SMALL?:
The legal size for crabs is 12cm/4¾in.

COMMONSENSE TIPS

CATCHING THEM:

1. TOOLS: Crab lines are simply rolls of string with a weight and a hook on the end, on which you attach a chicken neck, piece of bacon fat, or some other raw meat.

2. STRATEGY: Crabs in the British Isles can still be caught using baited crab lines dangled off the end of a harbour wall, or in a deep rock pool at low tide. Our children have spent many a happy hour catching crabs this way.

COOKED DRESSED CRAB

FRESH CRAB
MAYONNAISE (OPTIONAL)
WHITE-WINE VINEGAR (OPTIONAL)
LEMON JUICE (OPTIONAL)
SEA SALT AND FRESHLY GROUND BLACK PEPPER (OPTIONAL)

1. To cook the crab, pierce the crab through the shell in the small indentation under the tail with a screwdriver. This means that the crab will hang on to its appendages during the cooking process.

2. Put into simmering water, bring back to a simmer, and cook for 5 minutes.

3. Switch off and cool.

4. Remove to cool completely, with back shell uppermost, then refrigerate.

5. To dress the crab, prize the shell from the body, remove the stomach sack that will be in the back shell, then shell by pressing its mouth to loosen.

6. Remove all the spongelike fingers ('deadman's fingers').

7. Push out the dark meat, then remove the legs and claws at the bottom knuckle to expose the white meat in the body or honeycomb.

8. Break the claws into the three joints, and break off the thick bottom joint of the legs. Use a nut cracker to break the legs and remove legs with crab pick, and a small hammer to crack the end claws.

9. Cover the meat and refrigerate until ready to serve.

10. To serve the crab, taste first, before mixing the brown and white meats together.

11. To serve, you can add a little mayonnaise or white-wine vinegar or lemon juice, and salt and pepper.

12. To add extra flavour, try adding a sprinkling of paprika, a dash of Tabasco, or some finely chopped coriander, parsley or thyme.

SHRIMPS AND PRAWNS

CATCHING THEM:

1. TOOLS: Shrimp nets and a bucket.
2. STRATEGY: Head for rock pools, skimming the edges of the rocks with a shrimp net, and poking around in crevices and overhangs. Bear in mind that you can spend a whole morning collecting enough shrimps to make a saucerful of prawn cocktail for your efforts. Try putting a shelled limpet in the bottom of a net, and leave it in the rock pool. Wait for the prawns to go for the bait, then haul up the net

MOLLUSCS (OYSTERS AND MUSSELS)

WHEN:

The rule that oysters and mussels should only be harvested when there is an 'r' in the month makes some sense, but it is not a blanket rule. Molluscs breed from May to August, so the rule makes sense on conservation grounds. Also, as waters get warmer in the summer months, bacteria increase, and this can mean that the bivalves are less efficient at filtering out toxins. However, we have eaten mussels in July with no ill effects, but be your own judge.

COMMONSENSE TIPS

• Don't collect mussels and oysters near human habitation or near a sewage outlet.

• Make sure you wash them in clean water before cooking, and check that they are be closed (i.e. alive).

MUSSELS

Thick-shelled and barnacle encrusted, the mussels we picked have seen a bit of life, quite unlike the thin-shelled farmed version.

Wild mussels require a lot of cleaning and rinsing in fresh water – you have to be careful to remove the beard (the hairy root) and any other small stones or grit that might be attached to the shells, but it's worth the effort.

Collect mussels at low tide, when the fattest and juiciest mussels reveal themselves growing on the rocks or old timber. Pick only the biggest ones, using your thumb and forefinger to pull them off with a sharp tug.

SEA FORAGE STEW *Makes 8 servings.*

We 'cobbled together' this stew on a family camping trip in Galloway from a day of foraging on the beach. This serves eight people, and has the added benefit of only using one pot.

3 tbsp	EXTRA-VIRGIN OLIVE OIL
2 cloves	GARLIC, CHOPPED
1	ONION, OR SAND LEEK, CHOPPED
100ml/4fl oz	DRY WHITE WINE
⅓–½ bucketful	MUSSELS, WASHED, DEBEARDED AND LEFT TO SOAK IN FRESH WATER
1 large handful	SEA BEET, RINSED AND CHOPPED
1 large handful	ORACHE, RINSED AND CHOPPED
2 large	BAGUETTES

Brought with us: olive oil, garlic, onion, white wine, baguettes, large pot. Foraged: sand leek, orache, sea beet, mussels.

1. In the large pot, heat the olive oil, and sauté the onions and garlic gently until the onions are translucent, about 5 minutes.

2. Add the white wine, and cook for a few more minutes, until the wine is steaming hot, but not boiling.

3. Take the mussels out of the fresh water and add then to the pot, together with the sea beet and orache, and cook until the greens are wilted and the mussels are open, about 5 minutes. Discard any unopened mussels.

4. Ladle the mussels into large bowls with plenty of the liquid. Provide a large bowl for discarding the mussel shells.

5. Serve with plenty of crusty bread to mop up the juice.

CAMPFIRE MUSSEL AND MUSHROOM SPAGHETTI

Makes 4–6 servings.

This is a dish to prepare over a campfire or for a family pasta meal at home. We used field and horse mushrooms that we had found, but dried mushrooms work with this also. We used wild thyme, but parsley works well, too.

300g/10½oz	LARGE FIELD MUSHROOMS, SLICED, OR 8 slices DRIED PORCINI MUSHROOMS
1.8kg/4lb	FRESH MUSSELS, WASHED, DEBEARDED AND LEFT TO SOAK IN FRESH WATER
6 tbsp	EXTRA-VIRGIN OLIVE OIL
½	ONION, CHOPPED
2	GARLIC CLOVES, CHOPPED
500g/1lb	SPAGHETTI
	SEA SALT AND FRESHLY GROUND BLACK PEPPER
1tbsp	THYME, OR PARSLEY, CHOPPED

1. If using dried mushrooms, soak the mushrooms in warm water for 30 minutes.

2. Take the mussels out of the fresh water and place in a shallow saucepan, cover and stand over a moderate heat until the shells open, about 5 minutes. There is no need to put water in with the mussels, as they release enough juice to steam in their own juices.

3. When the shells have opened, remove the pan from the heat, and leave to cool slightly. Then pick the mussels out of their shells, remembering to reserve the mussel juice. Throw away any mussels that do not open. Strain the liquid, and set aside.

4. Heat three tablespoons of the olive oil, and add the onion, garlic and mushrooms, and fry gently until the onion is translucent, about 5 minutes. Add the mussels and about

mussels

half the juice, and heat gently for another 2 minutes.

5. Bring a large pan of water to the boil, drop in the spaghetti, and cook until al dente.

6. Drain the spaghetti, and transfer to the pan containing the sauce. Season with salt and pepper, and mix the sauce through the spaghetti.

7. Add the remaining three tablespoons of olive oil and heat through thoroughly.

8. Sprinkle with a generous serving of thyme or parsley, and serve.

WINKLES

Fiona has wisely retracted the statement 'life is too short to get your winkles out with a pin', as we reckon they are good additions to soups or stews.
WHAT:
Looks like a small black snail.
FIND IT HERE:
On the rocks; you should just be able to knock them off. Collect winkles off the beach. Winkles are easy to find, even if the bigger game are eluding you. The fatter, juicer ones are best, probably found nearer the low tide line.
NOTE:
Poach them, or add them to soups, or as an addition to a fish dish.

COMMONSENSE TIPS

• Winkles can be removed from their shells with a pin

WHELKS

WHAT:
Larger versions of winkles.
FIN IT HERE:
On the rocks; they are easy to find on any rocky beach. Common whelks live below the low tide line, but dog whelks are easily to be found in any rock pool.

COCKLES

WHAT:
Fan-shaped, small 2.5-centimetre (1-inch) smooth shells, extending to 7.5-centimetre (3-inch) horned ones, with ridges.

WHERE:
Cockle beds are usually localised to areas of wide, flat beaches around tidal estuaries. If you are lucky you will be able to pick them off the beach, alternatively, you can rake them out from a few centimetres below the surface.

CATCHING THEM:
TOOLS: A garden rake or any improvised raking device will do!

SEASHORE STOCK

This stock became the basis of a rich-flavoured seashore bisque (see recipe below).

We hadn't collected enough crabs and lobsters to eat as a stand alone meal, so we combined everything we had collected into a large pot, covered it with water, and simmered it for 30 minutes, to make a flavoursome stock. The pot contained a few crabs, some whelks and winkles, some dulse and carrageen, lovage and thyme, all collected along the seashore.

If you don't use it immediately, it can be frozen for use later.

SEAFOOD MAYONNAISE *Makes 4–6 servings.*

Add ingredients such as wild or cultivated garlic, rock samphire, sorrel and mint, as required.

2 large	EGG YOLKS
1 tsp	DIJON MUSTARD
	SEA SALT AND FRESHLY GROUND BLACK PEPPER
300ml/10½fl oz	EXTRA-VIRGIN OLIVE OIL OR COLD-PRESSED SUN-FLOWER OIL
Juice ½	LEMON

1. Put the egg yolks, mustard and salt and pepper in a food processor, and mix for a few seconds.

2. Keep the processor running smoothly and dribble oil in, in a thin stream continuously, until the mixture starts to form into a thick cream.

3. Add the lemon juice at the end.

CRAB CAKES *Makes 4 servings.*

The great thing about making crab cakes is that you can alter them according to who you are feeding and what time of day you are eating them. Make sure you get the ratio right: two parts crab to one part potato. For a more exotic variety, you can add lemon grass, chilli and Thai fish sauce, or you can just enjoy them plain or eat them with a tomato salsa or béchamel/watercress sauce.

500g/1lb	COOKED CRABMEAT (WHITE AND DARK MEAT)
250g/½lb	POTATOES, COOKED AND MASHED
1 medium-sized	SHALLOT, FINELY CHOPPED
1 tbsp	CORIANDER, FINELY CHOPPED
1	DE-SEEDED SWEET PEPPER, FINELY CHOPPED
	SEA SALT AND FRESHLY GROUND BLACK PEPPER
1	EGG, BEATEN
2 tbsp	PLAIN FLOUR
150g/5½oz	BREADCRUMBS
1 tbsp	EXTRA-VIRGIN OLIVE OIL

1. Place the crabmeat, mashed potato, shallot, coriander and sweet pepper in a bowl and mix together by hand. Add seasoning, and mix that in, too.

2. Divide the mixture and shape into eight cakes.

3. Coat each one by first dipping into the beaten egg, then flour then breadcrumbs.

4. Leave to cool for 40 minutes in the fridge.

5. When the crab cakes have cooled, heat the oil in a frying pan (preferably one large enough to cook them all at once), making sure the oil is moderately hot so that the cakes sizzle on contact. The cakes need about 4 minutes each side.

6. Serve with a salad or tomato salsa sauce.

SEASHORE BISQUE *Makes 4–6 servings.*

If you have any lobster/crabmeat, this can be added to the soup at the end of cooking, but this stands up with or without, provided the stock is good. The paprika adds an interesting kick to this creamy bisque. Serve with rounds of toasted country bread and a glass of dry sherry.

	LOBSTER/CRABMEAT (OPTIONAL)
60g/2oz	BUTTER, DIVIDED
30g/1oz	EXTRA-VIRGIN OLIVE OIL
1 large	ONION, CHOPPED
1 large	CARROT, CHOPPED
1 stalk	CELERY, CHOPPED
1 litre/2 pints	SHELLFISH STOCK
425g/15oz	TOMATO PURÉE
45g/1.5oz	FLOUR
60ml/2fl oz	DRY SHERRY
225ml/8fl oz	DOUBLE CREAM
	PAPRIKA (OPTIONAL)
	CHIVES, CHOPPED (OPTIONAL)
	SEA SALT AND FRESHLY GROUND WHITE PEPPER

1. If you are adding lobster/crabmeat, and are intending to cook live crustaceans, put them in the fridge or freezer before cooking to send them into a torpid state.

2. In a large stock or soup pot, melt one tablespoon of butter with the olive oil.

3. Add the onion, carrot and celery, and cook over a low heat for about 20 minutes, stirring occasionally, until soft but not browned.

4. Add the stock and tomato purée and simmer 20 minutes.

5. Strain the mixture through a fine sieve and return to the pot, measuring out 250ml/9fl oz and setting it aside.

6. If cooking live crustaceans, immerse your lobster or crab in boiling water, and boil – 12 minutes for 500g/1lb or 15 minutes for 750g/1½lb, with an extra 5 minutes for every additional 500g/1lb – then transfer it to ice water to cool quickly. Remove the meat from tails and

claws and discard shells. Cut meat into small pieces, reserving whole claw meat for garnish, if desired. Add any juices to stock.

7. Melt the remaining butter in a small saucepan over a low heat. Whisk in the flour and stir until smooth.

8. Very slowly, stir in the sherry and the reserved sieved liquid, then add this mixture to the large stock pot and bring to the boil, whisking until smooth. Reduce the heat, add the lobster/crabmeat, if required, and simmer for 10–15 minutes.

9. If you want to make a garnish, spoon a quarter of the cream into a small bowl, and mix in the paprika and chives.

10. When ready to serve, whisk the remaining three quarters of the cream into the bisque and season.

11. Ladle bisque into bowls and, if using, top with the reserved claw-meat pieces, and, if desired, garnish with the paprika and chive dressing.

GRILLED MACKEREL WITH GOOSEBERRY SAUCE
Makes 6 servings.

Gooseberries and mackerel go together like love and marriage. Mackerel is a hugely underrated fish, which is a pity, because it is cheap, easy to catch, and delicious if cooked fresh.

75g/3oz	BUTTER
750g /1lb 11oz	GOOSEBERRIES, TOPPED
225ml/9oz	AND TAILED
3 tsp	DOUBLE CREAM
	CASTER SUGAR
3	SALT AND FRESHLY
	GROUND BLACK PEPPER
3 tbsp	MACKEREL, FILLETED,
3 tbsp	SKIN ON, OR SIX MACK-
	EREL FILLETS
	WHOLEGRAIN MUSTARD
	OLIVE OIL

mackerel

1. To make the gooseberry sauce, heat the butter in a small saucepan, place the gooseberries into the pan, cover and cook over a medium heat for 20–25 minutes, until tender.

2. Remove the lid and mash the gooseberries lightly, then add the cream and sugar, season with salt and pepper, and continue to cook for a few minutes. Remove from the heat, cover and set aside to keep warm.

3. Preheat the grill to high. Brush the flesh side of the mackerel fillets with the wholegrain mustard, brush both sides with olive oil and season with salt and pepper. If you are using whole mackerel, smear the mustard inside the fish, and brush the outside with the oil and seasonings.

4. Place the mackerel skin-side up on a baking sheet and place under the grill for 4–5 minutes, or longer if using whole fish, until just cooked through.

5. Serve with gooseberry sauce, freshly boiled new potatoes and a green salad.

⚜ SUMMER SOLSTICE FEAST ⚜

21 June

———

Sea-caper Dip and Oatcakes
*

Crab cakes
Green Salad
*

Lobster bisque
*

Elderflower Fritters
Carrageen and Cinnamon Ice Cream

———

MUSHROOM SAFARI

8

{ Amethyst Deceivers, Boletes, Chanterelles,
Chicken of the Wood, Field Mushrooms,
Hedgehog Fungus, Horse Mushrooms,
Puffballs, Shaggy Ink Cap, Wood Blewit }

FORAGING FOR FUNGI

The mushrooms that we have included are the most commonly found and easily identified edible mushrooms, ones that you are unlikely to go wrong with if you follow the identification guide. If in doubt, don't pick.

More than just fun to find, some mushrooms are as rich in protein as meat or fish, and contain large amounts of minerals, such as iron, calcium and phosphorus, as well as vitamin Bs and D2.

Date: *1 September*
Place: *Grassland and mixed woodland*
Objective: *Edible mushrooms*

We had long known of George Peplinski's mushroom prowess, ever since he dated Fiona's sister – there's obviously something attractive about a man who knows his mushrooms. George, known as 'Pobble' for reasons lost to history, is a second-generation Polish immigrant, so mushrooming is in his DNA; he learnt his mushrooms from his parents in the woods near Leeds. Pobble and his wife Hazel embody 'The Good Life' – all vegetables are home grown, every surplus rabbit has been shot and skinned and made into stews, and there is nothing in this world that Pobble can't skin, bottle, pickle, stew, freeze or fix.

Pobble, like most mushroom-spotters, has his special places. We set off across the fields to see what we can find, in the opposite direction, we suspect, from his cep spot, which he has already told us he won't take us to. We head for a mixed woodland of pine and larch, where Pobble hopes a bounty of boletus awaits.

We decide to introduce some competition into the safari; a straight walk in the woods isn't cutting it for all of the junior male foragers. We tell them they will win an ice cream if they find five different kinds of mushroom. Lorne instantly drops the stick he has been wheeling around a younger boy's head, and walks off into the trees.

The more dedicated hunters crowd around Pobble for the first find of the day: a brown wood mushroom (**Agaricus silvaticus**), found under a pine tree. Pobble cuts the stem, which turns blood red; a positive ID – that goes into the basket.

Next, the children spot some yellow-capped mushrooms with spongy undersides, in woods, underneath the larch trees. The caps, poking out through the grass are slimy, and have grass and leaves sticking to them.

Our initial ID is Slippery Jack (**Suillus luteus**), but these are growing under larch, not pine, so we confirm them as larch bolete, (**Suillus grevillei**), which, as with Slippery Jack, have sticky caps. They share the spongy pores common to all boletes, (even though they are not technically boletes but suillus) and, while they are not the prize ceps, they're good enough for us, though we may peel them before cooking. Last year was a bounteous mushroom year, when we found horse mushrooms, chanterelle and masses of boletes growing in places that, this year, they are absent.

'I've found a different one!' shouts Lydia, standing guard over her specimen underneath a pine tree, just in case anyone else claims it as their own. Pobble confirms the ID as shaggy parasol (**Lepiota rhacodes**), which can cause a tummy upset in some people, but which we later eat with no side effects. The basket is filling up with larch boletes as we walk to the edge of the woodland, where it's Mungo's turn to add to the ice-cream tally: some horse mushroom (**Agaricus arvensis**) at the side of the field, which we confirm as such by scraping the base of the stem to check it doesn't stain chrome yellow.

Back home, Hazel is waiting with cake and juice and tea, equilibrium restored after two hours in the veg patch, as she shoves bags full of runner beans into our hands to take home.

Later, at home, we divide the spoils, and Xa makes hers into a mushroom ragout for the freezer, while I slice mine and dry them for the cupboard.

Commonsense tips.

danger

- Some fungi are very poisonous and some give you an extreme allergic reaction. Make sure that you are very sure of identification before you eat any of the mushrooms you gather. If in any doubt, don't eat – better safe than sorry!

- Even edible mushrooms can cause gastric upsets if you haven't eaten them before (one in fifteen people suffer gastric allergy to a new edible mushroom). Introduce new mushrooms into your diet gradually.

- Don't collect mushrooms alongside busy roads, as mushrooms absorb lead and other pollutants.

- Only collect from plentiful populations, and take no more than you can use for personal consumption (about 1.5kg/3lb per visit is recommended) and no more than half the fruit bodies of any single grouping of mushrooms.

- Always seek the landowner's permission before you enter land, and follow the Country Code, respecting any livestock.

- Mushrooms should not be picked for commercial reasons, unless previously agreed with the landowner.

- Do not collect 'buttons' (mushrooms that have not expanded). It is important to give the mushroom time to grow, so that it can spread its spores; also, there will be more to eat later!

- When picking a mushroom, hold the stem near the bottom and twist or cut with a sharp knife. This allows other fruits to grow in its place.

- Trim and clean off mud with a knife before placing the fungi in the basket.

- Do not collect species you do not intend to eat, and do not remove dead wood, apart for what you need for identification.

- Respect and protect all species, even the poisonous ones.

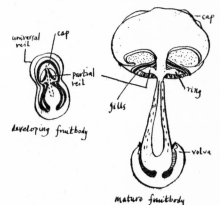

universal veil

cap

partial veil

developing fruitbody

cap

ring

gills

volva

mature fruitbody

Preparing mushrooms:

- Wipe dirt off, do not wash.
- Cut off any piece of mushroom that is soggy or soft.
- Check for maggots by slicing in half. Only use mushrooms which are in good condition and not too old.

Drying mushrooms:

- All boletes are good to dry, especially bay bolete and cep.
- Smaller mushrooms can be threaded on a string and hung up to dry.
- For larger mushrooms, spread out (preferably whole) thin slices on some newspaper, then cover with a cloth. Leave in a dry place, such as an airing cupboard or on top of a radiator, or, if the weather is hot, outside in the sun.
- Alternatively, they can be dried on a rack in the oven on a very low heat with the door open. Turn the mushrooms regularly; should take about 24 hours to dry.
- When dry, store in sealed jars or containers. Unsatisfactory slices can be turned into mushroom powder (good soup stock) with a mortar and pestle.

Freezing mushrooms:

- Good mushrooms to freeze are: chicken of the woods, hedgehog fungus, Chanterelles and boletes.
- Make sure only good specimens go in the bag, wiped clean.
- Don't overfill the bag.
- To defrost, plunge the frozen mushrooms into salted boiling water for a few seconds, then use as if fresh.

Pickling mushrooms:

- See Pickled Mushrooms in Brine recipe, page 147; or, for easy pickling, if you're in a hurry, you can use a good bought bottled dressing.

BOLETES

Members of this family are considered fine edible trophies, though their texture varies from firm to slimy and slippery, making some more prized than others. All boletes have spongy pores on the underside, making them easy to identify.

There are many different types, most are edible, and only one Satan's bolete (*Boletus satanus*) is poisonous, but, thankfully, it is extremely rare in the British Isles. It is a very solid and bulbous bolete with lurid red pores that bruise blue.

The bitter bolete (*Tylopilus felleus*) is not poisonous, it is just bitter, and, therefore inedible. This bolete has white pores when young – pink pores later – which bruise brown. It can be confused with the cep (*Boletus edulis*), but the cep has white pores that do not change colour when bruised. If unsure, try a small piece as a last resort and then spit it out if it tastes too bitter. Unless it is the Satan's bolete or the bitter bolete, and has a spongy underside, then you are OK.

CEP, PENNY BUN OR PORCINI
{*Boletus edulis*}

Arguably the most prized of the boletes, ceps are the most flavoursome of the group, with a sweet nutty taste.

IDENTIFICATION

WHEN:
June to November.
FIND IT HERE:
Near or in mixed woodland – coniferous trees, oak, beech, birch or chestnut – edges of golf courses and near heather.
WHAT IT LOOKS LIKE:
White swollen stems and brown bunlike heads, these mushrooms are easy to spot. The cap can be up to 20cm. White, firm flesh. Pores white, becoming greenish-yellow as they age, but do not change when bruised. (Remember, if it does change colour, it isn't a cep.) The stalk and cap merge into one when young.

COMMONSENSE TIPS

• Cut the fungi in half to check whether clean of maggots. Also, check staining on flesh to see whether colour alters. Avoid old specimens. It holds its flavour best when dried. Young ones can be eaten raw.

RED-CRACKED BOLETUS
{Boletus chrysenteron}

Commonly found. Best mixed in with other mushrooms as can go slimy. Its texture is not as firm as some of the other boletes, but still worth using. Smells fruity.

IDENTIFICATION

WHEN:
May to December.
FIND IT HERE:
Under broad-leaved trees, such as oak and beech. More often found in lowlands.
WHAT IT LOOKS LIKE:
Uneven hemispherical cap, which is olive brown in colour, revealing red-yellow flesh in the cracks. The pores bruise yellow to blue/green as they age. The thick stem is yellow, moving down to red/brown at the base.

COMMONSENSE TIPS

• Can disintegrate in cooking but, when dried, they can be crumbled into stews and casseroles.

ORANGE BIRCH BOLETE
{Leccinum versipelle}

This mushroom is very tasty and worth looking for.

IDENTIFICATION

WHEN:
August to November.
FIND IT HERE:
Under birch trees.
WHAT IT LOOKS LIKE:
Tall stemmed with orange to yellow-brown caps. Pores go from grey, to white, to yellow. The stem goes white, through purple to black, when cut.

COMMONSENSE TIPS

• Dries well. Don't bother eating the stems.

BAY BOLETUS
{Boletus badius}

Fairly commonly found, this boletus has a delicate sweet taste.

IDENTIFICATION

WHEN:
July to November.

WHAT IT LOOKS LIKE:
A glossy dark reddy-brown colour when moist. When dried out a little, it looks more leathery. Pores and tubes on the stalk are whitish, bruising greenish-yellow, then blue-grey to the touch. Has a stouter stem compared to its cap. Indistinctive smell. Small compared to other boletes.

FIND IT HERE:
Coniferous or deciduous woods, where there are open spaces under pine trees.

COMMONSENSE TIPS

• Collect only young specimens, where pores are not too dark green. This species is less maggoty than some others.

• Can be sliced thinly and eaten raw in salads. Dries well. Cooking uses similar to cep. Delicious lightly fried in butter with garlic and parsley.

SUMMER BOLETUS
{Boletus reticulatus}

This mushroom is up there with ceps as far as its sweet taste goes. It's of a similar size, though not very common.

IDENTIFICATION

WHEN:
June to November.

FIND IT HERE:
Likes beech and oak, as well as coniferous.

WHAT IT LOOKS LIKE:
Pale-brown top that becomes smooth and cracked as it gets older. Pores white to green-yellow. Stem is pale brown and mottled.

COMMONSENSE TIPS

• Dries well.

PICKLED MUSHROOMS IN OIL

This is a more extravagant way of preserving your mushrooms through the dark months. Our Polish friend is passionate about mushrooms in oil, eaten as an appetiser or with cold meats, or you can eat them straight out of the jar.

1kg/2lb	WILD MUSHROOMS
1	PLAIN OLIVE OIL (EXTRA-VIRGIN IS TOO RICH)
	SPRIG ROSEMARY, OR SMALL CHILLI PEPPERS OR SHAL-LOTS, THYME OR BAY LEAF (OPTIONAL)

BRINE:

600ml/21fl oz	WHITE-WINE VINEGAR
300ml/11fl oz	WATER
1 tbsp	SEA SALT
	BAY LEAVES
5 cloves	GARLIC

1. Clean and slice the mushrooms.

2. Combine all the brine ingredients in a pan and bring to the boil, then add the mushrooms, and boil for 10 minutes.

3. Using a sterilised spoon (see Pickled Mushrooms in Brine, Page 147) scoop the mushrooms out of the brine, and leave them to dry for a couple of hours.

4. Spoon a few mushrooms into a sterilised jar, and pour over a little of the oil, continuing in this way, alternating with mushrooms and oil.

5. If desired, for extra flavour, add the seasonings.

PICKLED MUSHROOMS IN BRINE

1kg/2lb **WILD MUSHROOMS**
½ tbsp **SALT**

BRINE:
300ml/11fl oz **WATER**
600ml/22fl oz **WHITE- OR RED-WINE VINEGAR**
1 **SPRIG FRESH DILL**
6 **BAY LEAVES**
4 **BLACK PEPPERCORNS**
1 clove **GARLIC**
4 **SHALLOTS**

1. Clean and cut the mushrooms into small pieces (the smaller the mushrooms, the better), cook in boiling salted water for 5 minutes, then drain.

2. Combine all the brine ingredients, and boil for 10 minutes.

3. Add the mushrooms to the brine and boil for another few minutes.

4. Using a sterilised slotted metal spoon (one that's just come out of the dishwasher, or has been heated in an oven for a few minutes), scoop the mushrooms out of the brine, and put into sterilized jars, making sure there is still room for the brine.

5. Boil the brine for another 5 minutes and then set aside to cool.

6. Strain the brine and pour into jars.

COMMON STINKHORN
{*Phallus impudicus*}

Its name, the common stinkhorn, or *Phallus impudicus*, about sums it up. Nature comes up with some pretty unusual and amazing creations, some so pretty they take your breath away, and others, such as the common stinkhorn, are amazing for completely different reasons.

Early on in my mushrooming days, I picked this mushroom thinking it might be an edible puffball. At the time, it was a round jelly ball with a leathery covering, smelling of raw peas.

I left it in the back kitchen overnight, to identify it later, not thinking that my procrastination would have such vile consequences.

Next morning, the house stank of rotting flesh. I searched the back of the fridge for meat I had forgotten about, then opened the door to the back kitchen to find, to my horror, a slimy, stinking white phallus with a glistening brown tip had erupted out of the jelly egg.

Apparently, the Chinese eat the jelly ball before it hatches – men for virility, women to get them in the mood.

CHANTERELLE
{Cantharellus cibarius}

This much prized mushroom changes hands for £25 per kilo (2lb) in delicatessens all over Britain. One of the most flavoursome mushrooms, they are relatively easy to find and identify, and need minimal preparation and cooking.

IDENTIFICATION

WHAT IT LOOKS LIKE:
Funnel shaped, with a convex cap when young, flattening out, with a central dip, and undulating golden, egg-yolk-coloured flesh. Ridges run from cap right down the stem. It measures 3–8cm (1–3in) tall and 3–10cm (1–4in) across. Has a fruity smell, faintly of apricots.

FIND IT HERE:
Commonly found under beech, birch or pine trees, or in open heath spaces with spongy moss.

WHAT CAN IT BE CONFUSED WITH?:
False chanterelle (*Hygrophoropsis aurantiaca*); grows in same areas, but is bright orange and the flesh is tougher, and doesn't have a fruity smell. Has gills, not ridges. Jack O'Lantern, (*Omphalotus olearius*) – very rare in Britain, only grows in Southern England on trunks and buried roots of sweet chestnut, oak and olive. It smells unpleasant. Gills that run down the stem and glow in the dark. Poisonous.

4. Spread the mushroom mixture over the pastry, leaving a 1-centimetre border all the way round.

5. Cook in a hot (400°F/200°C/Gas 6)oven for 15 minutes, or until the pastry has turned golden and risen.

6. Sprinkle with some extra flat-leafed parsley when it comes out of the oven, and serve warm or cold with a green salad.

JANE'S CHANTERELLES ON TOAST *Makes 4-6 servings.*

225g/8oz CHANTERELLES (AS MANY AS YOU CAN FIT IN A FRYING PAN)
1 ONION, FINELY CHOPPED
1 clove GARLIC CLOVE, FINELY CHOPPED
1 handful PANCETTA (PLUS MORE TO TASTE), FINELY CHOPPED
1 glass WHITE WINE
2 tbsp PARSLEY, CHOPPED
60g/2oz PARMESAN, FRESHLY GRATED
145ml/5fl oz DOUBLE CREAM

1. Wipe clean the mushrooms. Do not wash, because they absorb water.

2. Fry the onion for 5 minutes, until golden, add the garlic and cook for 1 minute, then add the handful of pancetta, and cook for another minute.

3. Throw the chanterelles into the pan. They will produce a lot of water, so boil down for a bit.

4. Add the wine, and boil down until there is just a bit of liquid left.

5. Throw in the parsley, Parmesan and stir in the cream.

6. Serve with bread or toast, is essential to soak up juices.

FIELD MUSHROOM
{Agaricus campestris}

HORSE MUSHROOM
{Agaricus arvensis}

These are the most common mushrooms growing in Britain. They are very similar looking, and are found growing in fields and pastures throughout the country from June to November.

IDENTIFICATION

FIND IT HERE:
Field mushrooms are found growing in grass, mainly on chalky soils, and in large numbers after rain. Horse mushrooms are found in fields and parks, especially where horses and cattle have been grazing, and occur in large groups.

WHAT IT LOOKS LIKE:
The field mushroom has a smooth, convex or flattened cap. The gills are deep pink, becoming chocolate-brown with age. The stems have a thin, fragile ring, and the stem is smooth about the ring, scaly below. The horse mushroom is egg-shaped, at first, then becomes convex and flattens out with age. The gills are white, when young, becoming pink then chocolate-brown with age. The stem is smooth, white, bruising a slightly faint yellow. As with the field mushroom, it has a white ring on the stem, though the ring is larger and less fragile than the ring on the field mushroom.

DON'T CONFUSE WITH:
Yellow staining mushroom (*Agaricus xanthodermus*). This poisonous cousin of the field and horse mushrooms grows in similar locations, but has important obvious differences. While the cap of the yellow stainer is white, both the cap and stem of this poisonous cousin bruise bright yellow when pressed. Also, unlike the field and horse mushrooms, the stem has a bulbous base, which, when cut, is chrome yellow. The mushroom has an unpleasant smell of ink when handled, and this smell intensifies on cooking.

HOW TO PICK:
Both field and horse mushrooms should be picked early in the day, as they are both prone to maggot infestation. The mushrooms often grow in the same location each year. Both mushrooms are excellent eating mushrooms, and dry well.

PARASOL MUSHROOM
{Lepiota procera}

This mushroom is both easy to identify and one of the tastiest. Called parasol because the mature specimens look like umbrellas on long elegant stems.

IDENTIFICATION

WHEN:
August to November.
FIND IT HERE:
Open spaces, within mixed woodland; grows in a scattered, haphazard fashion.
WHAT IT LOOKS LIKE:
The cap is shaped like a drumstick when young. Full-grown cap has concentric brown scales around the centre. White flesh underneath. The gills are white to off-white, broadly spaced like pages of an open book, and do not bruise to another colour. The stem is grey-brown and tall, with brown scales and a loose ring.
DON'T CONFUSE WITH:
Shaggy parasol (*Lepiota Rhacodes*). Some people have an allergic reaction to this mushroom. It looks similar to *procera*, but flesh turns orange-red when cut, and the gills bruise red-brown. The cap has a woolly texture

COMMONSENSE TIPS

• Excellent eaten fresh. Avoid washing, since it dilutes the flavour. Dries very well. Stem not worth eating.

HEDGEHOG FUNGUS, OR URCHIN OF THE WOODS
{*Hyndum repandum*}

Highly rated, this fungus is popular in markets in Europe.

IDENTIFICATION

WHEN:
June to November.
FIND IT HERE:
Coniferous and broad-leaved woods, near streams.
WHAT IT LOOKS LIKE:
Creamy-yellow body, wavy margin that curls under, depressed centre.

White spines under cap. Stem is short and thick and often off-centre, can grow conjoined, two or three together. Soft crumbly flesh.

COMMONSENSE TIPS

Remove the spines on larger specimens. Great with meat or fish. Good for drying or bottling in oil.

SHAGGY INK CAP, OR LAWYER'S WIG
{*Coprinus comatus*}

Easy to find, and tasty.

IDENTIFICATION

WHEN:
April to November.
FIND IT HERE:
Commonly in grass, by roadsides and on waste ground.
WHAT IT LOOKS LIKE:
Cylindrical fruit body, sausage-shaped when a button, slightly bell-shaped at base as it opens up. White, with brown top and covered in scales, making it look shaggy. The gills go from white, to pink to black, according to age. Stem tall and white with swollen base.

commonsense tips.

- Don't wait too long after picking before using, as quality deteriorates. Throw away if the gills turn black. Needs little cooking. Not suitable for drying. Cut stem from bottom with knife.

- Delicious rolled in egg and breadcrumbs. Also good in soups, stews and sauces.

WOOD BLEWIT
(Lepista nuda)

Easy to find and identify and good in the pot. The wood blewit is one of the later-ripening mushrooms. Easy to gather a decent amount because they grow in numbers.

IDENTIFICATION

WHEN:
September to December.
FIND IT HERE:
Mixed woodlands, gardens and hedgerows. Sometimes found growing in circles.
WHAT IT LOOKS LIKE:
Cap has a psychedelic tinge; lilac to blue through to tan. Large and flat when young, and as it matures it becomes more crinkly with a depressed centre. Gills lilac, but become pink-brown with age. The stem is bright violet, which with age becomes paler. Flesh bruises violet and fades to grey with age. Smells and tastes fruity.

COMMONSENSE TIPS

- First-time consumers only eat a small amount, as it has quite a strong taste and can be indigestible to some. Pick when dry, as can hold considerable moisture. Delicious incorporated in stews or casseroles, or simply fried in butter with garlic and parsley.

GIANT PUFFBALL
{Calvatia gigantean}

IDENTIFICATION

WHEN:
July to October.
FIND IT HERE:
Open fields and spaces.
WHAT IT LOOKS LIKE:
Large rounded shape, no stalk. The body has creamy-white flesh and has a good firm consistency.

COMMONSENSE TIPS

• Only eat when young and the flesh is firm. As it gets older flesh becomes discoloured and yellow.

GIANT PUFFBALL FRY UP

> BACON
> EXTRA-VIRGIN OLIVE OIL
> PUFFBALL, SLICED
> BUTTER
> EGG(s)

1. Fry the bacon in the oil and keep warm.
2. The puffball should be a clean white-looking mushroom. Fry the slices in butter and oil until golden in colour. Keep warm.
3. Fry the egg(s).
4. Serve like a piece of toast with bacon and egg on top.

COMMON PUFFBALL
{Lycoperdon perlatum}

This fungus should only be eaten when it is young and firm-fleshed.

IDENTIFICATION

WHEN:
June to January.
FIND IT HERE:
Commonly found among mixed woodland, growing among leaves.
WHAT IT LOOKS LIKE:
Small and creamy-white flesh when young, covered with little spines, with a circle of raised bumps around them. Flesh becomes more olive-coloured when mature.
DON'T CONFUSE WITH:
Earth balls, which are browny/grey with scaly, reptile-like skin, not milky white and smooth.

commonsense tips.

• If you are unsure about whether the puffball is still good to eat, tap on it – if it sounds hollow, chuck it; if it sounds dense, keep it.

• Puffballs are only worth eating when young. Great fried up with other mushrooms, they are also good in stews and casseroles, and as extra thickener for soups etc.

CHICKEN OF THE WOODS

{Laetiporus sulphurous}

IDENTIFICATION

WHEN:
April to November.
FIND IT HERE:
On trunks of trees, favouring oak and yew.
WHAT IT LOOKS LIKE:
Fan-shaped egg-yolk yellow on top, becoming pale and creamy when old. Grows in tiers, in pancake formation. Has the texture of chicken meat.

COMMONSENSE TIPS

• Best eaten young. Goes well in mixed-mushroom dishes.

MUSHROOM KETCHUP

Great for stews, mince dishes, sauces and gravies, adding more intensity of flavour.

2kg/4½lb **MIXED WILD MUSHROOMS**
SEA SALT
4 tbsp **FRESHLY GROUND BLACK PEPPER**
3–5 blades **MACE**
ALLSPICE BERRIES

1. Pick through and clean the mushrooms (with a knife, cut into the older ones to check if maggoty, and dispose of those that are).

2. Break up any large fresh mushrooms and put them into a large china bowl.

3. Cover them with salt and put them in cool place for 3 days, stirring regularly with a wooden spoon, and adding mushrooms and salt until you have decent quantity.

4. Strain the liquid into a saucepan and simmer for 30 minutes.

5. Add the black pepper, mixed spice and mace.

6. When the mixture is cold, strain, discarding the mushrooms, and put into bottles.

WILD MUSHROOM SOUP *Makes 6 servings.*

225g/8oz WILD MUSHROOMS (BOLETES, WOOD BLEWITS, CEPS, AMETHYST DECEIVERS, HORSE, FIELD MUSHROOMS ETC.)

½ litre/1 pint CHICKEN STOCK

½ litre/1 pint MILK

SEA SALT AND FRESHLY GROUND BLACK PEPPER

1 tbsp butter BUTTER

28g/1oz FLOUR

PARSLEY, CHOPPED

1. Pick through and clean the mushrooms (with a knife, cut into the older ones to check if maggoty, and dispose of those that are).

2. Pour with stock and milk into a liquidiser, season well, then liquidise.

3. Melt the butter in a pan, remove from heat, and stir in flour.

4. Gradually, add the liquidised mushroom mixture, and bring to the boil, stirring continuously, then reduce the heat and simmer for 10 minutes.

5. Add the chopped parsley, and serve with chunks of crusty bread.

WILD MUSHROOM RAGOUT *Makes 4 servings.*

This is a great recipe for processing a large amount of mushrooms. It is both quick and easy to make and will last for a few days in the fridge, or in the freezer for longer: up to two months for optimum taste, but it can be frozen for between 9 months and a year. Delicious eaten with papparedelle pasta or mixed into a risotto or simply with toast and butter and a green salad.

4 cups	ASSORTED BOLETES AND OTHER MUSHROOMS (PARASOL, FIELD, HORSE, CHANTERELLES ETC.)
3 tbsp	BUTTER
1 tbsp	OLIVE OIL
1 medium	ONION, FINELY CHOPPED
1 tbsp	FINELY CHOPPED GARLIC
125ml/4½fl oz	DRY RED WINE
250ml/9fl oz	CHICKEN STOCK
1 tbsp	DARK SOY SAUCE
1½ tsp	FRESH THYME, CHOPPED, OR ½ tsp DRIED
	SEA SALT AND FRESHLY GROUND BLACK PEPPER
1 tbsp	CRÈME FRAÎCHE (OPTIONAL)

1. Pick through and clean the mushrooms (with a knife, cut into the older ones to check if maggoty, and dispose of those that are), then cut into 1-inch chunks.

2. Heat some oil and butter in a heavy-bottomed pan.

3. Add the onion and garlic, and sauté on a medium heat, until translucent.

4. Add the mushrooms and cook for eight minutes until soft.

5. Add the wine and cook for 5 minutes or so, until the wine has reduced by half.

6. Add the stock, soy sauce and thyme, and simmer for 15–20 minutes, until reduced by half again.

7. Remove from heat, season, and swirl in some butter and a spoon of crème fraîche, if required.

BUTTERNUT SQUASH AND CEP SOUP *Makes 6 servings.*

This soup scores highly on taste and comfort factor. It can be made with
dried mushrooms if there are no fresh ones available.

3 tbsp	EXTRA-VIRGIN OLIVE OIL
85g/3oz	BUTTER
2 medium	ONIONS, FINELY CHOPPED
1.3kg/3lb	BUTTERNUT SQUASH, CUT INTO 2-INCH CUBES
	SEA SALT AND FRESHLY GROUND BLACK PEPPER
1 tsp	GROUND CUMIN
½tsp	GROUND GINGER
1 glass	DRY WHITE WINE
125ml/4½fl oz	CHICKEN OR VEGETABLE STOCK
300g/10½oz	FRESH CEPS (OR 55g/2oz DRIED)
handful	FLAT LEAF PARSLEY, FINELY CHOPPED
	CRÈME FRAÎCHE
	CROUTONS

1. In a heavy-based pot, heat the oil and butter over a medium heat and stir in the onions, then cover and leave to
   cook for 15 minutes, until translucent.

2. Add the squash, salt and pepper, cumin and ground
   ginger, and cook until the squash is soft, approximately
   15 minutes, stirring occasionally to check that the vegetables do not burn.

3. Add the wine, and let things simmer until much of the
   liquid has evaporated.

4. Add the stock, bring to the boil, then add the ceps, and
   cook for 10 minutes. Press down on some of cubes of
   squash, to obtain a thick soup.

5. Check the seasoning, add the chopped parsley, a swirl of
   crème fraîche and croutons.

BARLEY RISOTTO WITH WILD MUSHROOMS

Makes 6 servings.

This is a variation on the normal risotto. If there are no fresh mushrooms available, use Wild Mushroom Ragout (see Page 161), stirred into it and warmed through towards the end of the cooking.

110g/4oz	SEASONAL ASSORTED FRESH MUSHROOMS
2 cups	ORGANIC PEARL BARLEY, OR ARBORIO RICE
1 glug	EXTRA-VIRGIN OLIVE OIL
½	ONION, CHOPPED
1 clove	FRESH GARLIC, MINCED
1	BAY LEAF
850ml/1½ pints	GOOD MEAT OR VEGETABLE STOCK
½ tsp	FRESH THYME, CHOPPED
1 tsp	FRESH OREGANO, CHOPPED
	SEA SALT AND FRESHLY GROUND BLACK PEPPER
1 tbsp	PARMESAN REGGIANO, SHREDDED (OPTIONAL)

1. Pick through and clean the mushrooms (with a knife, cut into the older ones to check if maggoty, and dispose of those that are).

2. Place half the barley, in a dry medium-sized sauté or frying pan and toast the grains over a medium heat. Shake or stir the grains while toasting. This will take approximately 3–5 minutes, or until the barley is golden-brown and has a roasted-nut smell. When complete, take off the heat and remove the grains from the pan to stop the cooking process, and set aside.

3. Heat up the stock and keep hot.

4. Place a medium-sized saucepan over a high heat and add the olive oil to just coat the bottom of the pan.

5. Add the onion and garlic, and cook until just softened, about 2 minutes.

6. Add the mushrooms, and cook for an additional minute.

7. Stir in the toasted barley, the untoasted barley and the bay leaf.

8. Stir in 125ml/4½fl oz of the hot stock and reduce the heat to a simmer.

9. Add 125ml/4½fl oz of the stock to the mixture, stirring continuously, until the barley has absorbed all the liquid. Repeat the process, 125ml/4½fl oz at a time, cooking slowly, until the barley is tender, about 20–30 minutes.

10. Remove the bay leaf, stir in the thyme, oregano, salt and pepper and Parmesan, to season, and serve.

For further help with identifying mushrooms visit www.rogersmushrooms.com

9 BERRIED TREASURE

{ Blackberries, Blackcurrants, Blaeberries, Damsons, Elderberries, Gooseberries, Oregon Grape, Raspberries, Rosehips, Sloes, Wild Strawberries }

Not long ago, we bumped into a friend coming out of a supermarket with a punnet of perfect, large, shiny blackberries. 'What are you doing, Martha?' we enquired. 'You can pick them for free just round the corner!'

'Time is money,' Martha was quick to reply, and went on her way with her shopping bags.

It is easy to forget in the throes of the weekly shop, that there are rich berry pickings all over Britain. We know our woods and hedgerows are dotted with raspberries, gooseberries, blackberries and wild currants, and the heath and moorlands are carpeted with blaeberries, but what of our urban spaces?

We decide to take responsibility for our own seasonal produce, and check out local cycle paths, water byways, waste ground, city walkways, back alleys, to see what is growing around us. We decide, first of all, to reconnoitre the back alley in our neighbourhood, just yards from Martha's supermarket. Brambles are growing in abundance, elderberries, too, and rosehips galore.

If we had dug deep into Martha's bags, we may even have found rosehip syrup, as it is back on the shelves for the first time in thirty years. It was standard issue during the Second World War, when the government had school children picking rosehips, due to their high vitamin-C content.

We make a back-alley batch of cordial, a year's supply, and feed it to the children, dribbled over vanilla ice cream and carrageen pudding, smoothies, granitas, and even into porridge in the morning, with a dollop of cream, a legacy from childhood.

Next, we go for a bike ride down the cycle path. These urban spaces, far from being neglected and uncared for, are now wildlife corridors teeming with edible plants, and wildlife protected by conservation bodies, rubber-stamped by the government.

We pick a vast quantity of brambles (blackberries), along with apples. Their taste is slightly sharper than the cultivated varieties but, nonetheless, absolutely delicious, scoring highly on flavour. None of the cycle-path users seem to be remotely interested in picking, so there is a rich stock to be had. After half an hour of picking the blackberries, we have not even begun to make a dent. Later, we make crumbles and granitas, and there is even some left over for breakfast smoothies with yoghurt and honey.

We've worked out how to multitask, which is the best reason to get picking in the hedgerow – you can walk your dog, get some exercise, bag your fruit quota for dinner and provide your kids, if you have them, with free snacks.

BERRIES

In general, wild varieties of berries are superior in taste to the cultivated ones, but do not grow in such prolific quantities, so a little goes a long way. Treat them like caviar or oysters – to be savoured, or picked and eaten straight off the bush. In summertime, look for some of the wild varieties of the commonly cultivated berries.

SUMMER BERRIES
WILD STRAWBERRY
{*Fragaria vesca*}

This is a summer berry that grows in woodlands, grassland and scrub. The berries are smaller than the cultivated variety. Try infusing their leaves, which make a tea that is delicate and fragrant.

RASPBERRY
{*Rubus idaeus*}

Wild raspberries have a wonderful flavour. Like most wild fruits, this is the plant that the cultivated one is descended from, and their taste is infinitely more subtle. You may not find them in prolific quantities, but they are delicious added to cereals, and sprinkled on top of yoghurt or ice cream.

raspberry – blackberry
blaeberry mushroom

GOOSEBERRY
{Ribes uva-crispa}

The wild gooseberry grows in woodlands and hedgerows everywhere. The light green, round, hairy berries have a 'tail' at the end of the fruit. They are excellent in desserts, and we have combined gooseberries with meadowsweet, a plant that grows in wetlands in the summertime, to make a delicious cordial.

BLACKCURRANT
{Ribes rubrum}

This little black berry really packs a punch and is widespread in woodlands and hedgerows throughout Britain, often, like the other berries, as a garden escapee. The leaf can be infused to add flavour to other herb teas or made into sorbets or cordials.

BLAEBERRY
{Vaccinium myrtillus}

The blaeberry (Scotland), bilberry or whortleberry (England and Wales), or frocken (Ireland) is a low-growing shrub that has pink flowers and small, pea-sized dark purple fruits, and grows on damp moorland. Unfortunately, Britain's large deer and sheep population enjoys blaeberries, so they are best found on moorland that is not grazed!

Blaeberries, like blueberries, their cultivated cousins, have superb antioxidant properties that guard against 400 named infections in both the intestine and urinary tracts. Blaeberries have been used to improve the health of the gut and as a cure for kidney stones since the 12th century. At Soutra Aisle, a large Medieval field hospital run by Augustinian Canons, south of Edinburgh, over 700 blaeberry stones were found during excavations of the ancient drains.

More tart than the blueberry, they lend themselves well to crumbles, cranachans, syrups or jams, or, in summer, granitas.

BLAEBERRY SMOOSH *Makes 4–6 servings.*

This dish is very quick to prepare and preserves the goodness and freshness of the blueberries, since there is no cooking involved. Serve in individual glasses, if preferred.

200g/7oz	AMARETTI BISCUITS
4–6 tbsps	VIN SANTO, OR OTHER SWEET WINE
500g/1lb	BLAEBERRIES
225ml/8fl oz	WHIPPING CREAM
250g/9oz	MASCARPONE
250g/9oz	CRÈME FRAÎCHE
4 drops	VANILLA ESSENCE
200g/7oz	SOFT DARK-BROWN SUGAR

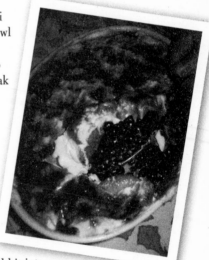

1. Spread the amaretti biscuits out in a bowl and pour the Vin Santo over them, to soften. Leave to soak for half an hour.

2. Meanwhile, wash the blaeberries, and pick out any twigs leaves etc., then place in the bottom of a medium-sized glass bowl or trifle dish.

3. Whip the cream, fold it into the mascarpone and crème fraîche, then mix in the vanilla essence.

4. Arrange the moistened biscuits over the berries, and spoon the cream topping over them.

5. Sprinkle the sugar over the cream in a thin layer, making sure the top is covered completely.

6. Serve immediately.

CRANACHAN *Makes 6–8 servings.*

This is a classic, unashamedly Scottish, dessert, which smacks of deca-
dence and good times. Coincidentally, it was on both our wedding-feast
menus. It is great with raspberries, wild strawberries, blueberries, any ripe
soft fruit really. And it couldn't be easier to make.

30g/1oz COARSE OATMEAL
500ml/17½fl oz DOUBLE CREAM
4 tbsp DRAMBUIE OR WHISKY
750g/1½lb SOFT FRUIT
SUGAR TO TASTE
MINT LEAVES

1. Toast the oatmeal in the oven, until lightly browned and
   crisp – but make sure it doesn't burn.
2. Whip the cream, until stiff, and stir in the alcohol.
3. Wash the fruit, and pick out any twigs, leaves etc.
4. Mix the oatmeal with the cream, add the fruit, and
   sweeten to taste.
5. Serve the cranachan in 6–8 large wine glasses, or in a
   glass bowl or trifle dish, and garnish with mint leaves.
6. Serve the cranachan soon after making, or the oats will
   go soft.

AUTUMN HEDGEROW BERRIES

Flopsy, Mopsy and Cottontail, who were good little bunnies, went down the lane to gather blackberries.
– The Tale of Peter Rabbit, Beatrix Potter

BLACKBERRY, OR BRAMBLE
{*Rubus fruticosus*}

Brambles, like nettles, need little introduction. Most people have, at some time, slipped a blackberry into their mouths as a late summer or early autumnal treat. They grow prolifically in hedgerows and along pathways everywhere. The first fruit at the tip of the cluster is the best to eat raw and the first to ripen. Later, the berries become seedy and are best used in jams and jellies.

SMOOTHIE *Makes 1 serving.*

Apart from them tasting great, here are some good reasons for starting off the day with a berry smoothie. Smoothies are great for using up bashed or overripe berries, and are great with frozen berries.

Blackberries are a useful source of vitamin C and contain salicylates (natural aspirin). Good for boosting the immune system, fresh blackberry juice is an all round tonic.

Raspberries are a rich source of vitamin C and a good antioxidant, great for cleansing and detoxifying the digestive system.

Blaeberries have superb antibacterial properties and help ease the digestion.

Instead of yoghurt, you can use vanilla ice cream, soya milk or regular milk. Experiment a little – that's the fun of it!

100g/3½oz FRESH WILD BERRIES (BLACKBERRIES, RASPBERRIES, BLUEBERRIES), OR FROZEN BERRIES
2 tbsp NATURAL GREEK YOGHURT
1 tbsp HONEY

1. Mix everything in a blender, and drink fast before someone asks you to make another!

PILTON PUDDING (OR AUTUMN PUDDING)
Makes 4-6 servings.

This is an autumnal version on the classic summer pudding, using brioche instead of white bread. We called it Pilton Pudding in honour of an urban part of Edinburgh, famous to fans of the book Trainspotting, where we picked berries along the cycle path to make this pudding. Beauty and Bounty can be found in unexpected places, even in the middle of a city.

700g/1½lb MIXED AUTUMN FRUITS (SUCH AS BLACKBERRIES, ELDERBERRIES, RASPBERRIES, APPLES)
110g/4oz SUGAR
8 slices BRIOCHE (PANETTONE CAN BE USED IF YOU CAN'T FIND BRIOCHE)
6 tbsp WATER
MINT LEAVES AND/OR FRESH FRUIT, FOR GARNISHING

1. Grease a 1-litre (2-pint) pudding basin.
2. Wash and pick through the fresh fruit, removing any stalks etc.
3. Put the water in with the sugar and fruit, and stew on a medium heat until it is soft but still retains its shape, then drain, putting the juice to one side.
4. Dip the brioche slices in the juice, and line the pudding basin with it.
5. Pile the fruit into the basin, making sure not to include too much juice, layering it with the brioche and ending up with a piece of soaked brioche on top.
6. Cover with foil, then place a saucer on top, and leave overnight in the fridge.
7. Run a knife around the inside of the basin to loosen.
8. Pour the excess liquid over the pudding before serving with double cream or vanilla custard.
9. Decorate with mint leaves and/or any extra autumnal fruit.

VENISON WITH BRAMBLE SAUCE *Makes 6–8 servings.*

900g/2lb **VENISON , EITHER BONED SADDLE OR FILLET**
5–6 **JUNIPER BERRIES, CRUSHED**
3 **SPRIGS OF THYME**
2 tbsp **HAZELNUT OIL, OR EXTRA-VIRGIN OLIVE OIL**
1 tbsp **EXTRA-VIRGIN OLIVE OIL**
60g/2oz **BUTTER**
1 large glass **RED WINE**
600ml/1¼ pints **MEAT STOCK**
60g/2oz **FRESH BRAMBLES (OR 1½ TBSP BRAMBLE JELLY)**

1. Cut the venison into steaks, approx 5–10 millimetres thick, and put aside.

2. Mix the crushed juniper berries, thyme and hazelnut oil, pour it over the venison, then cover and refrigerate for 1½ hours, to marinade.

3. If you are using fresh brambles, cook them with a little sugar, until soft, then push them through a sieve, remembering to save some berries for garnish.

4. Heat the olive oil and half the butter in a frying pan, sear the steaks quickly on each side, and reserve the pan juices.

5. Arrange the steaks in an ovenproof dish, and cook for 5–10 minutes in a moderate oven (350°F/180°C/Gas 4).

6. Meanwhile, add the wine to the reserved pan juices and reduce by half, then add the stock and reduce again.

7. Add the fruit purée (or bramble jelly) to the pan, followed by the rest of the butter, then season and mix well.

8. Serve the venison, with the sauce poured over it, with creamy mashed potatoes and braised red cabbage with apples, or green beans.

BLACKBERRY CORDIAL

450ml/1 pint WHITE-WINE VINEGAR
1.14 kg/2½lb RIPE BLACKBERRIES
450g/1lb SUGAR
225g/8oz HONEY

1. Pour the white-wine vinegar over the blackberries, and leave to stand for one week, stirring occasionally.
2. Strain when ready and put liquid into a pan with the sugar and honey.
3. Bring to the boil, then cool.
4. Bottle and keep in dark place.

FRUIT AND BERRY CRUMBLES *Makes 6 servings.*

This has to be the quintessential winter food. The classic crumble can be adapted, using any fruit that is available, and nuts, oats or other cereals can be added to the topping mixture for a little bit more variety. Adapt according to what is growing, and what you have in the cupboard. Here are some ideas: bramble and apple; elderberry and apple; rhubarb and elder-flower; gooseberry and meadowsweet; damson and pear.

BASIC TOPPING:
175g/6oz PLAIN FLOUR
80g/3oz CASTER SUGAR
50g/2oz BUTTER

FOR VARIATION, ADD:
SPICES (SUCH AS ½ TSP GROUND GINGER AND I TSP CINNAMON)

OR NUTS
APPLE AND CHOPPED WALNUTS OR PECANS, APRICOTS AND GROUND ALMONDS

AND CEREALS
1 cup ROLLED OATS
1 cup CORNFLAKES
1 cup GRANOLA

1. Butter a pie dish.
2. Prepare your chosen fruit, then put in the dish and sprinkle sugar on top.
3. Combine the crumble ingredients in the food processor
4. If desired, mix in whatever spices, nuts or cereals you've chosen.
5. Spread the crumble mixture on top of the fruit, and bake in a preheated oven, at 350°F/180°C/Gas 4, for 30–40 minutes. Dab the top of the crumble with extra butter if it looks like burning.

ELDERBERRY
{*Sambuca nigra*}

The elder grows prolifically in hedgerows, on waste ground and in woodlands throughout Britain. It is one of the most useful shrubs, its blossoms the source of early summer cordials, its fruits ripening in September and October. The dark purple fruits of the elder are ripe when they start drooping downwards in a dense cluster on a reddish stem.

An invader species, the red-berried elder (**Sambucus racemosa**), introduced by foresters and planted at the edge of, or on, plantations after clear cutting, should not be picked, as the berries are toxic.

Eaten raw in quantity, the elderberry can be slightly toxic, but they are an excellent addition to any fruit pudding, and make a great purée for sorbets and ice creams, as well as an excellent cordial and syrup. Try elderberry compote as an accompaniment to strawberries and cream in the summer. The taste is not unlike blackcurrant.

commonsense tips.

- The easiest way to pick elderberries is to snip off whole bunches of berries. At your leisure, you can then strip the berries off the stem using the prongs of a fork.

- The flowers, leaves, bark, roots and fruits of the elder all have medicinal qualities. Elderberry syrup is a storehouse of vitamins A and C, great for taking out of the cupboard in winter to keep colds, flu and sore throats at bay. Until the end of the 19th century, elderberry drinks were sold on the streets of London on cold winter days to lend workers some cheer. Try it hot, with cinnamon or honey.

ELDERBERRY ICE CREAM *Makes 4 servings.*

½ carrier bag-full **ELDERBERRIES, PICKED FROM STALKS**
SUGAR, TO TASTE
Juice ½ **LEMON**
225ml/8fl oz **DOUBLE CREAM**
2 **EGG WHITES**

1. Put the elderberries into a saucepan with a little water and a sprinkling of sugar, and the lemon juice. Go steady on the sugar, you can always add more later, if you need to.

2. With a lid on the saucepan, gently simmer for about 45 minutes, or until the elderberries have gone very soft.

3. Remove from the heat and leave to cool, then push the berries through a sieve. Taste the syrup, and add more sugar, as required. This will make about a pint of syrup.

4. Whip the cream until it stands in peaks.

5. In a separate bowl, whisk the egg whites until they are stiff enough to tip the bowl upside down.

6. Fold the cream, egg whites and elderberry syrup together gently, until the whole mixture is a uniform colour.

7. Pour into a suitable freezer container and freeze.

ELDERBERRY SYRUP

450g/1lb **ELDERBERRIES, PICKED FROM STALKS**
450g/1lb **SOFT BROWN SUGAR**
1 **EGG WHITE, BEATEN**

1. Rinse the elderberries in cold water, drain thoroughly and crush them.

2. Put into a heavy-bottomed saucepan with the sugar, and bring slowly to the boil, skimming off any scum.

3. Simmer, until it reaches the right syrupy consistency.

4. Stir in the egg white, to help clear the liquid.

5. Strain through muslin, cool, then pour into sterilised bottles with stoppers or screw tops.

6. Store in a cool dark place.

OREGON GRAPE
{*Mahonia aquifolium*}

This immigrant from North America was a
favourite of the Native American Indians, this
shrub is now planted in gardens and parks,
and is naturalised in woodlands. You may
have walked past it in your local park without realising it is edible. The grapes are best
left on the plant to ripen, and picked later
on in the season. Like elderberries, they are
best cooked and put through a sieve.

ROSEHIP
{*Rosa canina*}

These red fruits are from the wild rose, and are common in hedgerows
throughout Britain. Rosehips have 20 times the vitamin C of oranges and,
during the Second World War, the Ministry of Health devised a rosehip
collection scheme. Making rosehip syrup was part of the war effort to keep
the country healthy, rosehips being collected in vast quantities throughout
that time.

commonsense tips.

• Rosehip Syrup (see recipe below) is great on
porridge, over ice cream and pancakes, or added to
smoothies. We serve it drizzled over carrageen pudding, and one of our favourite uses is ice cold with
vodka for a naughty little cocktail!

ROSEHIP SYRUP

3.5 litres/6 pints WATER
1.5kg/3lb RIPE ROSEHIPS, SLICED
1kg/2l SUGAR

1. Pour 2.5 litres (4 pints) of the water into a heavy-bottomed pan, bring to the boil, then drop the rosehips in.
2. Bring back to boiling point and cook for 30 minutes, skimming while cooking.
3. Strain through a muslin or jelly bag, retaining the liquid and boiling the pulp with the rest of the water.
4. Cool for half an hour, then strain through the jelly bag once again.
5. Combine the liquids and boil until reduced further, then add the sugar and bring to the boil.
6. Cook until smooth and syrupy, then cool and pour into sterilised bottles.
7. Store in a dark cupboard or fridge.

SLOES

These small, round, plum-coloured fruits come from the blackthorn, and are best picked after the first frosts. They are acidic, so best made into jellies or, most famously, sloe gin.

Blackthorn is widespread and abundant throughout the British Isles in hedgerows and woodland. Be careful, though, as blackthorn has hard prickles; so use gloves to pick the sloes.

DAMSONS

Asmall dark fruit, hard to touch, black skin and green flesh, the newer variety are larger and more rounded. The smaller older fruits have a better flavour. Found in old gardens, orchards. Trees sometimes look grey and twisted.

MARY RUNDELL'S SLOE AND APPLE JELLY

This recipe also works with damsons, using the same proportion of apples to damsons.

2.7kg/6lb WINDFALL APPLES, SLICED AND CORED
1kg/2lb SLOES
WATER
SUGAR

1. Put the apples and the sloes into a jam pan, barely cover with water, and simmer gently until all the fruit is soft and pulpy.

2. Strain through a jelly bag, then return the juice to the pan together with the sugar, allowing 1lb of sugar to each pint of juice. Stir until the sugar has dissolved, then return to the heat and boil until the setting point is reached.

3. To test for set, remove the pan from the heat, then place a few drops of the jelly on to a cold plate, and allow to cool. If the jelly has formed a skin that wrinkles when a finger is pushed gently into it, then the jelly will set. If this doesn't happen, boil the jelly for a little longer and retest.

4. Pour into clean hot jars and seal with lids, or covers, immediately.

5. Store in a dark cupboard.

DUCK BREAST WITH DAMSONS *Makes 4 servings.*

500g/17½oz DUCK TRIMMINGS (WINGS, NECK, CARCASS)
2 CARROTS, PEELED AND COARSELY SLICED
2 SHALLOTS OR 1 SMALL ONION, COARSELY DICED
1 clove GARLIC, CUT INTO 3
1 SPRIG THYME
1 BAY LEAF
250g/½lb DAMSONS
200ml/7fl oz BURGUNDY
25g/1oz BUTTER

20g/½oz CLARIFIED BUTTER

4 DUCK BREASTS, EACH WEIGHING ABOUT 350g/12oz

1 pinch SUGAR

SEA SALT AND FRESHLY GROUND BLACK PEPPER

1. To prepare the sauce, coarsely chop the duck trimmings, put into a fireproof roasting dish in the oven for 20 minutes, until lightly browned.

2. Remove the tin from the oven, set over a moderate heat, add the carrots, shallots, garlic, thyme and bay leaf.

3. Reserve 100g/3½oz of the best damsons, then add the remainder to the roasting dish, and cook for 2 mins, then add the red wine.

4. Turn up the heat, bring to the boil, stirring briskly, scraping the base and sides of the roasting dish with a wooden spoon.

5. Pour in sufficient cold water to cover the bones, bring to the boil, adjust to a gentle simmer, and cook for 30 mins.

6. Pour the stock into a large sieve and set over another pan.

7. Return the strained stock to the heat, boil until reduced to a syrupy consistency then gradually whisk in the butter. Taste, season and keep warm.

8. To cook the duck, heat the clarified butter in a frying pan over a high heat.

9. Fry the duck breasts, skin side down, for 3 minutes, then on the other side for 5 minutes (they will be very pink). Wrap in foil and reserve to keep warm.

10. Pour off the fat from the pan and return to the heat. Add the reserved damsons and a pinch of sugar. Heat for a minute, then sprinkle on to the surface of the warm sauce and continue to keep warm.

11. To serve, slice the duck breasts very thinly, lengthways, trimming away any fatty skin, then arrange the slices in a fanned-out rosette on four warmed serving plates. Spoon some damsons into the centre of the rosette or around the sliced duck. Coat the meat with the sauce and serve immediately.

SILVY'S SLOE AND WINDFALL APPLE CHEESE

This is a good complement to cold meat, particularly game, and hard cheese, eaten with oatcakes or crusty bread. You can try using different moulds. It makes a change from quince, and the colour is rich and deep. The apples can be a mix of cookers and eaters.

1.2kg/2½lb APPLES
275ml/½ pint WATER
900g/2lb SLOES
SUGAR

1. Cut up apples without peeling or coring them, but discard any bruised bits.

2. Put into a preserving pan with water and simmer until the apples are soft and broken down.

3. Add the sloes and continue simmering until they are soft.

4. Rub through a sieve and weigh the purée, then, over a low heat, stir in the sugar until it has dissolved completely. Allow 450 grams (1 pound) of sugar for every 450 grams (1 pound) of purée.

5. Bring to the boil and simmer, stirring well, until the mixture is thick, which will take about an hour.

6. Pour into clean hot jars, and cover.

7. Store in a dark cupboard.

DAMSON/ SLOE GIN/VODKA

Mix the sloes/damsons with half their weight of brown sugar, and half fill empty bottles with the mixture.

Pour the gin or vodka over, and seal tightly. Store for at least two months, and shake occasionally, and it will be ready to enjoy by Christmas.

Roger Banks, an eccentric forager friend, used to keep his sloe gin bottles underneath the back seat of his car so that they would get a regular gentle shaking!

WILD DAMSON CREAM *Makes 6–8 servings.*

1.5kg/3.5lb DAMSONS (OR OTHER WILD FRUITS)
     WATER
     SOFT LIGHT-BROWN SUGAR
250ml/8floz GREEK YOGHURT
250ml/8floz LOW-FAT YOGHURT
120ml/4floz WHIPPING CREAM

1. Put the damsons in a saucepan, barely cover with water, and simmer until the flesh is so tender that it falls off the stones.

2. Sieve the pulp, weigh it and return to the pan with three quarters of its weight in sugar.

3. Simmer until all the sugar is dissolved, then set aside and allow to cool.

4. For a yoghurt cream, stir together the two yoghurts and pour them into a colander lined with three or four layers of muslin, set over a bowl, and leave it to drain for several hours. You should end up with a thickened yoghurt with a sour-cream texture.

5. Beat the whipping cream into the bowl until it starts to hold some shape, then add 55g/2oz of icing sugar, and continue beating until it holds its shape.

6. Beat in the drained yoghurt, then fold in the damson or wild-fruit purée, stirring thoroughly.

YUMMY MUFFINS *Makes 12 muffins.*

Any available fruit can be used in these muffins, whatever is close to hand and ready picked. Blaeberries, raspberries, blackberries and elderberries are all good options.

300g/10oz PLAIN FLOUR
175g/6oz SUGAR
1½ tsp BAKING POWDER
½ tsp BAKING SODA
1 pinch SEA SALT

90g/3oz CREAM CHEESE
Juice of ½ LEMON
2 tsp VANILLA EXTRACT (VANILLA ESSENCE)
2 EGGS
4 tbsp HOT MELTED BUTTER
125ml/4½fl oz MILK
1 cup BERRIES (OF CHOICE)

1. Combine the flour, sugar, baking powder, baking soda and salt in a mixing bowl, stir well, then set aside.

2. In an electric mixer, process the cream cheese, lemon juice and vanilla extract, until smooth.

3. Add the eggs, and process for 15 seconds.

4. Pour in the melted butter, then process for another 10 seconds.

5. Add the milk and mix.

6. Add the dry ingredients to the mixing bowl and mix through.

7. Add fruit, and mix through in pulses, or fold in if you want your berries whole.

8. Pour an equal amount of batter into each muffin cup in the tray, ideally filling it to about three-quarters full.

9. Bake for 30 minutes.

. . . .

SHORTBREAD *Makes 32 slices.*

It is easy to add a little extra taste to this classic biscuit by substituting a drop of cordial – elderflower, rosehip, strawberry etc. Take out 1 tablespoon of sugar and substitute 1 tablespoon of syrup instead.

225g/8oz BUTTER
110g/4oz SUGAR
375g/12½oz SIFTED FLOUR

1. Cream the butter with the sugar, then add the flour, until well combined.

2. Chill the mixture.

3. Pat into two 18-centimetre (7-inch) circles.

4. Place on baking sheet and mark 16 wedges in each, then bake at 300°F/150°F/Gas 2 for 30 minutes.

5. When cooked, sprinkle caster sugar on the top, while still hot.

WILD FRUIT GRANITAS *Makes 6 servings*

Granitas probably trace their origin back to Roman times, though this dish was popularised by the Arabs.

1kg/2lb RIPE FRUIT (BLACKBERRIES, RASPBERRIES, BLAEBER-
RIES, ELDERBERRIES ETC.)
150g/5oz ICING SUGAR (OR MORE FOR MORE ACIDIC FRUITS)
LEMON JUICE TO TASTE, ACCORDING TO HOW SWEET
THE PULP IS

1. Smoosh the fruit through a sieve to get rid of the pips.

2. Mix in the icing sugar, stirring until the sugar has melted. Adjust using lemon juice until you have the correct sweetness.

3. Pour into a shallow pot or tub (the mixture should be no higher than ¼ inch) and freeze until the outside is solid. Check every 40 minutes.

4. Smash up frozen puree with a fork and re-freeze.

5. Repeat at least twice more before eating. This should all be done over a two hour period.

6. When the mixture is completely frozen, fluff up with a fork, put back in freezer for a further half hour, then pile up in tall glasses – go for the full effect.

7. Garnish with mint or citrus zest.

HEDGEROW JAM

A great way to use up smaller quantities of fruit. Kids love collecting and identifying all the different berries.

225g/8oz ROSEHIPS
225g/8oz HAWS
225g/8oz ROWANBERRIES
225g/8oz SLOES
500g/1lb CRAB APPLES, CHOPPED
500g/1lb BLACKBERRIES
500g/1lb ELDERBERRIES
113g/4oz HAZELNUTS

1. Wash all the fruit well. Put the rosehips, haws, rowanberries, sloes and crab apples into a pan, then add water to cover, and cook until tender.

2. Sieve and weigh the pulp.

3. Put the pulp into a pan with the blackberries, elderberries and chopped nuts, and simmer for 15 minutes.

4. Add 1kg (2lb) sugar, plus the weight of the pulp in sugar.

5. Cook over a low heat, until sugar has dissolved, then boil rapidly, until the setting point is reached (drop teaspoon of jam into saucer of iced water to see if it has set).

JELLIES AND JAMS COMMONSENSE TIPS

- When you embark on making a batch of jam/jelly, make sure you sterilise at least half a dozen jars, especially if you have a lot of ripe juicy fruit.

- It depends which fruit you are using as to how much juice is yielded, and how many pots you end up with.

- 1.3kg/3lb sugar makes about 2.3kg/5lb jam.

❧ HARVEST SUPPER ❧

Wild Mushroom Risotto
*
Venison fillet with Bramble Sauce
Mash
Braised Red Cabbage with Apple
*
Windfall Apple and Elderberry
Crumble

❧ KIDS HARVEST LUNCH ❧

Mushroom Soup with Dulse Soda
Bread
*
Elderberry Ice cream

~Blackberry~ elderberry
~Raspberry~ ~rosehip~

ACKNOWLEDGEMENTS

Firstly, thanks to the supporting cast in this book for all their enthusiasm: our husbands, Duncan Wood and Simon Milne, and our children, Adair and Lydia Wood, Geordie, Lorne and Mungo Milne.

Chris Watt, freelance photographer, who has been dragged up hills, down muddy banks, through rock pools, heavy cameras in tow, in search of an elusive plant or a great camera shot, with unfailing good humour.

Thanks to our illustrator, Olivia Doherty, who has illustrated this book beautifully at very short notice, and her husband Mark.

Dr. Brian Moffat, our ethno-biologist, who we adopted as our academic expert, and with whom we have enjoyed many outdoor ethno-botany tutorials, and learnt so much.

And to Pawel Orzechowski, our Man Friday, who has taken on everything from childcare to computer support to cooking and even translation services, and without whom multitasking would have been impossible.

Thanks to our agent, Stan, of Jenny Brown Associates, for all his support and good humour.

Thanks to our foodie friends who have helped us with advice and information: Melissa and James Fergusson, Alex Renton, Carolyn Rann, Jane Raven, Sylvie Weatherall, Sarah MacAlpine, Mary Rundell.

To Kate Botting, Lulu and Matthew Benson, Richard Bath, Claire and Frazer McCready, Miles and Louisa Nelson, Tamsin Oglesby, Jeremy Salvesen, William Milliken, Finn MacCreath, Mooie Scott, Jane Laing, Robin Nicholson, Rachel Barne, Val Houston and all the other friends that have provided, sometimes unwittingly, material for this book.

With thanks to the men who helped us learn bushcraft: Duncan Wood, Simon Milne and Jeremy Hastings, Islay Birding and Bushcraft.

Nick Roper Caldbeck of Garroch Glen Environmental Tours (www.garrochglen.com) for a memorable day of foraging and tree spotting.

Thanks to Roger Banks, David and Maria Chamberlain, Rosalind Burgess, Willow Walker, Margaret Horn and the countless other people we have interviewed in the course of writing this book. To Roy Watling and Valvona & Crolla for a great fungal foray, and to David Mitchel and the Northern Ireland Fungus Group for the use of their mushroom identification pictures.

Thanks to Casilda Grigg and the editors at the Weekend Telegraph for all their support, and to Ali Gunn for her help in pushing us onwards.

Thanks to Carolyn Thorne, Gareth Fletcher and the team at Virgin for their enthusiasm and hard work.

Finally, thanks to our parents, Moira and Adair Houston, Gavin and Elizabeth and Diana Younger for introducing us to our love of nature, food and the freedom to explore.

SOURCES, REFERENCES AND FURTHER READING:

Beedell, Suzanne: *Pick, Cook and Brew*, Pelham Books, 1973

Burrows, Ian: *Food from the Wild*, New Holland, 2005

Cooper, Marion R and Johnson, Anthony W: *Poisonous Plants and Fungi in Britain*, Stationery Office Books, 1998

Craighead, FC Jr and Craighead, JJ: *How to Survive on Land and Sea*, U.S. Naval Institute Publication, 1943

Elliot, Rose and de Paoli, Carlo: *Kitchen Pharmacy*, Chapmans, 1991

Fergusson, James, *The Vitamin Murders – Who Killed Healthy Eating Britain*, Portobello, 2007

Harding, Patrick, Lyon, Tony, Tomblin, Gill: *How to Identify Edible Mushrooms*, Collins, 1996

Hartley, Dorothy: *Food in England*, Macdonald & Co. (Publishers) Ltd, 1954

McIntyre, Anne: *Healing Drinks*, Gaia Books, 1999

McNeill, Marian F: *The Scots Kitchen*, Mercat Press, 1929

MacNicol, Mary, *Flower Cookery*, Collier-MacMillan, 1972

Mabey, Richard, *Food for Free*, Collins, 1972

Milliken, William and Bridgewater, Sam: *Flora Celtica – Plants and People in Scotland*, Birlinn Ltd, 2004

Phillips, Roger, *Wild Food*, Pan Books, 1983

Richardson, Rosamond, *Hedgerow Cookery*, Penguin, 1980

Symson, Andrew, 'A Large Description of Galloway', 1710

Wiseman, John, *SAS Survival Handbook*, Collins Harvill, 1986

INDEX

Education Policy Perspectives:
School Organization and Improvement Series

General Editor: Ivor Goodson, University of Western Ontario, Canada

Series Editor: David Reynolds, University College, Cardiff

Education in general and schools in particular are at the forefront of public debate in most industrialized societies. Only a decade ago, there was a pervasive belief that education 'didn't matter' and that educational reform and expansion as attempted worldwide in the 1960s and 1970s would inevitably produce failure and disillusionment.

Now, however, the work of academics, practitioners and policy-makers in the effective schools movement shows that schools can generate excellence *and* equity if they are run in certain ways. School improvement researchers and practitioners are also showing how schools can be made more effective and efficient.

This series aims to bring to the attention of teachers, administrators, policy-makers and academics the latest research, practice and thinking in these fields. It aims to stimulate academic debate about school effectiveness and improvement, and to provide practitioners with the detailed analysis and description of effective school strategies that they need as societal and legislative pressures on schools grow even stronger. Now more than ever before, educationists need to know about 'good schools' and about 'how to make schools good'. This series aims to provide just that information.

Improving the Quality of Schooling
Edited by David Hopkins

The Comprehensive Experiment
David Reynolds and Michael Sullivan with Stephen Murgatroyd

The Self-Managing School
Brian J. Caldwell and Jim M. Spinks

Successful Secondary Schools
Bruce L. Wilson and Thomas B. Corocoran

Whole-School Approaches to Special Needs: A Practical Guide for Secondary School Teachers
Edited by Arlene Ramasut